Leading Change, Overcoming Chaos

Leading Change, Overcoming Chaos

**A Seven Stage Process
for
Making Change Succeed in Your Organization**

by

Michael Heifetz

Threshold Institute

1🕭
Ten Speed Press
Berkeley, California

1⊜
TEN SPEED PRESS
P.O. Box 7123
Berkeley, CA 94707

Cover and text design by Stephen Herold

Library of Congress Cataloging-in-Publication Data on file

ISBN 0-89815-591-6

FIRST PRINTING 1993
Printed in the United States
1 2 3 4 5 — 97 96 95 94 93

Personal Note from Michael Heifetz to readers of this book:

I hope the ideas in this book help you successfully manage change in your organization. I'd appreciate your telling me what parts of this book were most useful.

In the next edition of this book, I'd like to include your tips and suggestions for making change happen. If I include your ideas, you'll get full credit, or remain anonymous if that is your preference.

In addition, Heifetz, Halle and Associates offers a variety of practical tools to help companies change, including seminars, customized workshops, educational materials, and consulting services.

If you'd like more information, or if you're reporting on your experiences with change, call me at (206) 866-1242, or write me in care of Threshold Institute, P.O. Box 10250, Olympia, WA, 98502.

Acknowledgments

This book owes a great deal to many people who have influenced my thinking about change. Several people with whom I have worked should be mentioned: Mihaly Csikszentmihalyi, Charles Krone, and James Liebig have provided guidance as well as their distilled wisdom about change and human motivation.

I'd like to credit several sources which have provided a background for the development of the Change Cycle. The concepts of driving and restraining forces were used by social scientist Kurt Lewin in the analysis of what he called force fields. I have been exposed to a three-force concept (thesis, antithesis, synthesis) through G.W.F. Hegel, the works of G.I. Gurdjieff (*The Law of Three*), and as a consulting associate of Charles Krone.

The idea of basic energies defining states of being has been used in Eastern philosophy and metaphysics, and well as by modern writers such as John Bennet. Arthur Koestler describes stages of the creative process in his book *The Act of Creation*.

There are also whole bodies of literature and research that have influenced me, including general systems theory, organizational development, dialectical theory, conflict models of creativity, and stage-based models of human development.

I wish to express my gratitude to the clients of Heifetz, Halle and Associates who have provided practical insight and feedback on how to use these ideas effectively. Also, thanks to my colleagues and associates who were advance readers of the final manuscript and shared many valuable suggestions for improving this book. Thanks to Cher Stuewe- Portnoff for editorial assistance.

There are two people who have encouraged me and stuck by me during difficult times while I grappled with these ideas. Stan Halle has not only been a steadfast friend, but has extensively field tested the Change Cycle model with our organizational clients. My wife, Laurel, has been a continual source of understanding and editorial insight. She has always maintained a delicate balance between supporting and challenging me. I hope this book is worthy of their confidence.

Table of Contents

Roadmap to This Book

Suppose you could focus an organization on a worthy change objective, sustain commitment to the change effort, overcome the inevitable resistance and practical hurdles, keep the implementation on track, and reach the point where the change itself becomes the norm and its benefits are tangible. Imagine completing one change and leveraging your organization's new confidence and capability to launch an even more ambitious change effort.

Unfortunately, most change efforts do not fare so well. Change initiatives may start with great enthusiasm, visibility, and upper-management support—but often die out before the goal is reached. Sometimes the effort gets bogged down in implementation; sometimes management attention or commitment wavers; perhaps day-to-day issues and priorities interfere. Maybe the organization doesn't buy into the need or the value of the change, or right in the middle of one effort, another gets launched.

Sometimes an organization holds on to its way of doing things, regardless of the risk in doing so, even to the point of self-destruction—going out of business, losing credibility with clients or constituents.

Leading Change: Overcoming Chaos was written for managers in business and government who are responsible for making change succeed in their organizations. This book is intended to help you:

- Effectively target a change
- Plan a straightforward path to accomplish your change
- Create a conducive climate for change
- Avoid or solve problems along the way
- Realize all the benefits of the completed change

Field Testing the Change Cycle

For almost twenty years, as an internal and external consultant, I have tried to understand how to achieve lasting change in organizations. My business partner and I have worked with organizations large and small to manage a wide variety of change efforts. Working with these clients gave us the opportunity to participate in successful change efforts, and to deal with the problems that often prevent changes from developing and stabilizing. Certain characteristics of successful change leaders and their methods became clear. We also began noticing recurring patterns in the way successful changes developed. These insights led to a description of how change evolves through seven distinct stages. I call this the Change Cycle.

The utility of the Change Cycle has been extensively field tested. It has proven to be a valuable tool for clarifying what needs to be done to achieve change and for alerting managers to typical roadblocks. The Change Cycle can help you become more effective in leading change.

Three Real-Life Examples of Change Cycle Successes

Let me share three examples in which we used the Change Cycle in successful change efforts:

A few years ago, as they tried to cope with escalating costs and shrinking margins, a large Midwestern transportation company was facing layoffs of approximately twenty-five percent of their salaried work force. We were called in to help identify ways to reduce costs while saving as many jobs as possible.

Applying the Change Cycle model, the client chose two specific targets:

(1) aggressively reduce non-labor based costs (e.g., fuel, systematic vehicle routing)
   and
(2) start a dedicated fleet business that would absorb excess capacity—an option that could provide very healthy margins.

First, the management team created a detailed vision of what the future state could look like. They used this company-wide vision to stimulate department heads and their teams to develop departmental versions of the vision and to activate cooperative changes. As the changes began to take shape throughout the company, the Change Cycle was used to anticipate, avoid, and solve problems at each stage of the process. The results were excellent:

- The dedicated fleet business got off to a promising start.
- Real operating cost savings were identified and captured.
- Only two people lost their jobs.
- The company went from having a weak position (typical for the industry) to having a competitive edge.

A $900 million military supplier was facing major work-force reductions, as forecasts of dramatic cuts in defense funding became a reality. Like other defense contractors, this company had to figure out a way to operate profitably at a much lower volume. The manufacturing management team was stuck due to the intense emotional burden of anticipating thousands of layoffs. They also could not imagine how to trim over sixty percent of their capacity and survive financially.

We used the Change Cycle model to help them break through their block. First they had to work through their strong emotions. Then they were ready to conceptualize what their business could look like in the future—smaller and more efficient, with a diverse international customer base, but still viable and profitable. This was a far more acceptable situation than the one they had been dreading. Even though layoffs were inevitable, the business could not only survive, but might even thrive. When managers compared this future state to their current situation, many became excited. Once their target was clarified—and believable—they began to sketch out a plan to transform their organization. Results: the team is currently well on its way toward the target. In fact, they are ahead of schedule.

An $85 million manufacturer of food sterilizers used in large food-processing facilities had successfully made a culture shift from an autocratic organization of 500 plus people to one that embraced continuous improvement and employee empowerment. Through the use of improvement teams, they had streamlined manufacturing processes and significantly reduced scrap and rework. The improvements to date had been piecemeal and internally focused, but product quality, delivery, and costs had been positively affected by the changes. Despite these successes, management noticed a gradual fading of enthusiasm and wondered what to do next.

Using the Change Cycle model, we pointed out that the current cycle of change had exhausted itself. The organization needed to step back, reflect on its accomplishments, consolidate what had been learned, and use that as a foundation for considering new possibilities.

By going through the wrapping-up stages of the Change Cycle, this company identified new capabilities that could be leveraged to address a current challenge—flattened markets in the U.S.A. They had proven that they could effectively upgrade their manufacturing process. This capability could be valuable in reshaping their operation to penetrate the European market. The target selected was to get "ISO 9001" certification. This is considered a prerequisite for manufacturers to become preferred suppliers in Europe. To accomplish this, their improvement teams—already in place as part of the old change effort—needed to be refocused on a common purpose: certification. This would require a series of process, documentation, reporting, and quality control changes that would pass muster with the official auditors.

Even though this target represents a big challenge, the organization has responded with enthusiasm and confidence, born of their previous successes in implementing change. The Change Cycle is currently being used to plan this initiative.

Benefits of the Change Cycle

Understanding and managing the Change Cycle improves your chances for successful implementation of any desired change. You can gain more control of the change you are trying to create, and of changes that occur around you. By applying this methodology, you can realize benefits like these:

- Successfully plan and implement new initiatives, and troubleshoot change in process.
- Anticipate problems and develop solutions that work for your unique situation.
- Maintain your balance and objectivity during the complex challenges that normally accompany change.
- Make lasting changes, and avoid regression to less effective patterns of the past.

Versatility of the Change Cycle

The seven-stage Change Cycle process can be applied to virtually any situation in which you or others are trying to make a change succeed. Here are a few examples of such applications:

- The Minister of the Interior of a South American country wishes to secure a policy change regarding preservation of the rain forest.
- A managing director of a nonprofit hospital is trying to change the way her institution interfaces with the medical community, neighborhood clinics, and a nearby teaching hospital.
- A planning team leader is assigned the task of figuring out what it will take to be a viable supplier of telecommunications equipment after the industry shakeout is over.
- A small high-tech company is about to merge with a much larger company. The CEO must deal with accomplishing the merger itself, as well as with issues concerning the incompatibility of the two organizational cultures.
- A mid-level manager in a governmental agency tries to assess why a recent procedural change was rejected in her office.

As you can see from these examples, the Change Cycle can be applied in a wide variety of situations. The uniqueness of each situation clearly affects how you manage the change. However, you are much more likely to achieve your goals if you understand the forces affecting any change process. It is here that this book can make the difference.

Leadership Versus Chaos

Leading Change: Overcoming Chaos was chosen as the title for this book because of the fundamental dynamic tension that exists throughout any organizational change effort. This is the tension between two opposing forces: Leadership and Chaos. Leadership, on the one hand, is the force which drives the change. Chaos is the resisting force which must be overcome or reconciled in order for the change to be completed. The force of Chaos takes many forms throughout the change process, but can always be recognized as resistance to the desired change. The term Chaos is used to connote the complex and powerful nature of the resistance to change, as well as its unpredictability.

Because of the powerful resistance any change effort faces, there is an overriding need for strong, able leadership. In order for it to work, someone must supply the initial activating force, the vision of what the change should look like, the wisdom and skills to guide the ongoing effort, and the perseverance to see the job through in the face of a continuing stream of problems.

In any change effort, leadership capability is pitted against formidable opposition—Chaos is not too strong a term for this opposition. There is quite a bit of inertia to overcome before any change effort can get started. Entrenched attitudes and values, habits, formalized procedures, existing skills, and personal preferences can all be inertial factors resistant to change. But inertia is only one of the barriers any change effort will face. As the change process takes form and begins to move through predictable stages, a continual stream of challenges will inevitably arise. The cost of the change in time, money, and required effort represents both initial and ongoing resistance to the forces driving the change. Along the way there may also be competitive activity which interferes with your process. There may be economic forces at work on an industry or national level that add complexity and frustration to your change effort. The marketplace may inject its own resistance to the desired change. There may be technical problems with new systems and procedures that crop up and stymie your best efforts. Internal political opposition may undermine the process, or simply defocus the effort.

Some of these challenges can be predicted and planned for, while others will be unexpected. The leadership will have to find ways and means to address all of these issues effectively in order to sustain movement toward their goals. This requires all the strategic, analytical, political, technical, and creative skills leadership can muster. It also requires a high degree of focus and commitment, for these challenges will not yield easily.

The importance of leadership within the change process is hard to exaggerate. Similarly, it is difficult to deny that leadership requires quite a diverse and well-developed skill set. Unfortunately, this rare set of abilities is often missing in organizations, regardless of size. The ideas in this book can enhance leadership skills by providing valuable tools to augment existing skills and talents. Several critical leadership capabilities are discussed here, and methods are presented to develop them. Examples and discussions are filled with useful principles, perspectives, insights, and techniques which can improve leadership capability. These examples have been chosen not only to clarify the Change Cycle, but to stimulate your thinking about actual day-to-day leadership issues.

The subject of leadership is not so much highlighted as a separate topic as it is embedded throughout the book. Almost every example given and point discussed is directed at the leader or the potential leader. You can also extend practically all of the ideas discussed to a general point of view on how to lead organizations, not just change efforts. In addition to the general leadership skills discussed, the Change Cycle itself is a powerful tool in the right hands. Once you can effectively manage change, you will be able to better manage a wide variety of other problems. In short, mastering the skills discussed here can substantially enhance your leadership capability, regardless of the challenge you face.

Road Map to This Book

The book is divided into two sections, each of which has a particular focus. Section I, Change Cycle Management: Practical

Understanding And Implementation, emphasizes hands-on management of change initiatives.

Chapter One introduces the Change Cycle by first discussing each of the seven stages in detail, and then providing an overview of the entire Change Cycle, using a chart to show the typical actions, barriers, and desired outcomes for each stage.

Chapter Two illustrates the application of the Change Cycle to a major change effort in a troubled fictional company, Cunningham Aviation. The stages of the cycle are identified as you follow Cunningham's story. At each stage, the story narrative is followed by a brief review of what has happened and its significance in the change process. By following this complete Change Cycle, you can gain a sense of how the cycle evolves in practice, what typical objectives and activities to expect in each stage, and the common problems that you can expect to face implementing change.

Chapter Three focuses on the individual stages. I've used examples in the form of short stories followed by brief discussions to highlight important barriers and problems typical of each stage.

Section II, Approaches To Managing Change, concentrates on management strategies.

Chapter Four concentrates on special issues in managing Change Cycles. Here I discuss the most helpful observations and practical usage suggestions I've gleaned from my management and consulting experience.

Chapter Five covers the pros and cons of forcing change by imposing your will on others and examines the costs and by-products that should be considered before choosing this method.

In Chapter Six, our focus is on political barriers to change, whether this resistance arises from deeply held beliefs or some form of self-interest; I share some ideas that can help to defuse politically charged opposition to change.

In Chapter Seven, humane methods of achieving change are discussed. Our focus is on techniques that are useful in gaining support and commitment to a change effort, so that the change is driven by the will of the participants as well as that of their leaders.

In Chapter Eight, intuition is introduced as an important tool for solving problems that arise during a Change Cycle. I discuss methods to access your intuition and creative problem solving ability.

An appendix is included for those who are interested in the theory behind the Change Cycle. This section is not designed for practical utility, but for those who would like to understand more about the concepts used in the rest of the book.

Suggestions for Using This Book

The most thorough understanding will be gained by reading the whole book. In fact, as you wrestle with the practical problems of leading a change effort, you may find it useful to come back to the book to look up information specific to your needs. It is, however, possible to glean what you most want by reading only the sections pertinent to your needs.

If your primary interest is in guiding a change process, including hands-on management, the quickest approach is to read Section I—an explanation of the stages and implementation advice.

If you are mainly interested in understanding the basics of the Change Cycle and the suggested approach to managing change efforts, but are not primarily interested in hands-on management of an implementation effort, you can read the explanation of the Change Cycle in Chapter One, then jump to Section II, the discussion of management approaches and general methods.

SECTION I

Change Cycle Management: Practical Understanding and Implementation

Chapter 1
Framework for Change

Deciding to Take Charge of Change

Change is inherent in life. We face constant change at work and home, and we live in a rapidly changing society and world. Change is neither good nor evil; it simply is. Change is part of the natural order of birth, death, and transformation. To ignore its presence is to downplay an aspect of life that gives vitality, purpose, and meaning to each of us.

Change is as natural a part of our creations as of ourselves, for change is intimately tied to creativity. In order to create any product, we must exercise our own vision, will, and capability toward the realization of something new. The vision is changed into a reality—a product of the change process.

We have a simple choice regarding change. Either we can let it operate on its own, affecting our lives as it will, or we can choose to manage change as best as we can. By accepting change as a natural process and choosing to manage it, we're really choosing life over entropy. By exercising our will, we become a creative force in the change process instead of letting it run its own course. By choosing to manage change, we're choosing to use our will and capability to create the kind of life we desire. We're selecting health and vitality over chaos and entropy. Consciously driven change is the essence of the creative transformation of life. To deny this is to deny a part of ourselves.

On a practical level, when we choose to manage change, we begin to establish a healthy environment for growth and a vital existence. Over time, those who choose to make change management central in their lives will experience a zestful, creative awakening. For most people, this rebirth must be experienced to be understood fully, but it can be glimpsed if you imagine going from a life of relatively static, predictable patterns, interrupted sporadically by a jolt of unwanted change, to a life filled with creative strivings. While change impacts all areas of our life, this book focuses on change in organizational settings.

Recognizing the practical benefits of establishing change management as a way of life isn't difficult. In business, change management assures that new products, services, and technological innovations are continually being developed. This outlook is more compelling and pervasive than simply having a research and development function in the organization. Rather, conscious change management is like having a whole organization full of people thinking about improvements, large and small, and about how to make those improvements real. Once an organization has this outlook as part of its being, change is looked upon as desirable and healthy rather than as something to be feared and avoided if possible. The strength, vitality, and long-term viability of a creative organization working toward improvements on a wide variety of fronts are hard to overstate.

Orientation to the Change Cycle

The model presented in this book, the Change Cycle, proposes an underlying structure inherent in all change processes, whether you are designing a new manufacturing method, preparing a bill for the legislature, reorganizing staff responsibilities, planning a merger, or trying to overcome a personal habit. This seven-stage model can be used to explain many different types of change, as long as that change is directed by conscious will. The seven stages of the Change Cycle are:

◆ Stage One: Choosing the Target
◆ Stage Two: Setting Goals

- Stage Three: Initiating Action
- Stage Four: Making Connections
- Stage Five: Rebalancing to Accommodate the Change
- Stage Six: Consolidating the Learning
- Stage Seven: Moving to the Next Cycle

Each of the seven stages of change has its own purpose and characteristics. In each stage, some significant smaller change must take place to propel the cycle forward. These smaller changes build upon each other, until the cycle is complete. There needs to be sufficient motivation and sustained effort to push a change through all seven stages to completion.

Understanding the flow of organizational change through the cycle, as well as the issues characteristic of each stage, will help leaders plan and implement change more effectively. For example, a common mistake people make when managing change is to assume the change is complete before it is. Another is to assume there is adequate commitment, when the commitment is actually far too weak to withstand the challenges any important change must face. Another is the failure to measure and feed back tangible preliminary results and benefits of the change while the change is still being established. As you become acquainted with the seven stages of change, you'll understand why organizational change is so often short-lived. More important, you'll learn how to direct change that endures.

Stage One: Choosing the Target

Most often, a change process is initiated when an individual or group feels discomfort or pressure. The source of the discomfort can be either internal or external, but frequently change seems to be stimulated by external sources. Such external sources of discomfort include changes in market or economic condition, competitive situations, technology, environment, and government regulation, as well as the expectations of society. Although less common, internal sources can also be compelling. For example, the changing expectations of employees regarding their appropriate roles in the organization can be an effective stimulus. Painful stimuli, while disturbing, actually increase our receptivity to the idea of change. While the desire for change can be linked to recognized opportunity, discomfort is more often the motivating factor. Once receptivity to change is established, the Change Cycle can begin.

The first question to answer in any change effort is whether or not the change is worth doing. Your question might be: "Given this organization's overall situation at this time, should this project be given priority as a discrete endeavor, or should it be included with related activities or functions?" The purpose of the first stage of any change effort is to allow for its existence. Is the project a high enough priority to warrant the assignment of money, staff, and other resources for its probable completion? If you decide to go ahead, then the change effort will take on a life of its own.

During the first stage of the Change Cycle, "Choosing the Target", your organization's change leadership will be identifying, evaluating, and selecting among alternate possibilities for responding to the factors that motivate your change effort. You might choose to leave things basically as they are. If things are going well enough, why change?

Changes that matter are those that offer true potential for your organization to progress in areas that are important to it, for example:
◆   Increasing profits
◆   Increasing effectiveness in carrying out public policy
◆   Strengthening your competitive position
◆   Improving service or customer relations
◆   Improving your product line
◆   Penetrating existing markets or expanding into new ones
◆   Becoming more cost-effective
◆   Increasing internal effectiveness
◆   Increasing employee job satisfaction

Such possibilities can generate a great desire for change, especially when coupled with a painful stimulus to initiate change. When the potential for these kinds of changes is clearly recognized within your organization—if the potential generates real interest—you have reason to continue. But if the alternatives fail to generate a sufficient level of initial commitment from your leadership, your change process will likely stall.

Once you've completed the process of selecting a target, the next step is to clarify, formulate, and refine your idea. What corporate, agency, or departmental direction are you talking about? Will this be a major shift in organizational focus, or are you refocusing on what you've intended to be doing all along? By taking this particular direction, what other directions are you not taking? Can you define a general target for what you wish to accomplish? Once the target is reached, what will it be like in your organization and for its constituents, customers, or clients?

Such questions should be asked regardless of the scale of the change under consideration. Begin to describe what the organization might look like once the change is fully integrated. What will the operational results look like? What jobs will people be doing? How will it feel to work there, once the changes become part of everyone's daily work life? What impact will these changes have on interactions and relationships among the divisions of your organization?

By the end of the first stage, a small core group will have selected and defined a target. Traditionally, this core group was composed of managers, but increasingly it is composed of employees at all levels who are intimately familiar with the functions requiring change. This work can be accomplished by a single person, but there is a real advantage to building a core leadership group early in the Change Cycle. The work of the first stage can go even further by defining a vision of the future that is based on the desired effects of the changes. By the time the targeted change is defined clearly enough to begin exciting belief and commitment in others, the work of Stage One is complete.

Stage Two: Setting Goals

The second stage of the Change Cycle is the time during which change leadership typically expands and gives greater definition to the purpose, scope, desired outcomes, and implementation plan for the change effort. During this stage, if not before, a design, planning, or implementation team is often formed. While this team will likely interact with others, much of their work will be done independently. Staffing this team cross-functionally can help give the planning effort a diversity of viewpoints and expertise, particularly from those divisions most directly affected by the change. If modifications are being made to an operational system, for example, include people from operations, engineering, marketing, and information systems on the team. It is especially important to include this cross-functional expertise at this stage, because the team is still relatively insulated during this period. It is also critical to tap outside sources, such as customers and independent subject matter experts, during this stage. Failure to integrate this external perspective can lead to serious misdirection of your change effort.

This planning team will be asking and answering a wide range of questions. These questions will range from broad assessments of the organization's capabilities, to critical analysis of the likely impact of the change on products, policies, priorities, customers, and internal systems. Also important are detailed inquiries into where resistance to change will likely crop up. The planners must gather and analyze all the relevant information at their disposal through whatever means are available.

One of their key tasks is to try to anticipate the major stumbling blocks they will face, and to determine how the potential problems will be addressed. It is a time when all the outrageous objections to the change should be raised and addressed as well as possible. It is a time when analysis and intuition are used to chart a course through all the known obstacles confronting the change, and a readiness to face unknown challenges is created.

Notice that many of the issues just mentioned came up in Stage One, as well. The difference in the assessment process in Stage One versus that in Stage Two is one of emphasis, specificity, realism, and completeness. In Stage One, the emphasis is on identifying potentially valuable changes to pursue. Questions asked tend to be broad and directional in nature. Information used in assessing possibilities may be sketchy, anecdotal, conjectural, and colored by the pain that stimulated receptivity to the change in the first place.

But in Stage Two, a closer scrutiny of the change takes place. More and better information is examined. Pitfalls are exposed. Questions of how much time, effort, and expense must be weighed against the potential benefits of the change. The will of the organization is given a more severe test now, as the resource level needed for the project becomes clearer. Your organization should either assure the resources required to accomplish the goals of the project, or reconsider its position with respect to those goals. The project may be redefined at this point or dropped altogether.

And so a choice must be made. Do we commit fully to reaching our target? Do we redefine our target, goals, and plan? Or do we back away from the project altogether? In Stage Two, one of the most important objectives is for the organization to test its will to see the project through. What was true in Stage One, "Choosing the Target", is just as true in this stage. Your project may or may not prove capable of moving forward to the next stage. All of us know of change efforts that have languished in these early stages of development. Quite a few are killed off in Stage One, before they're even given project status. Others never gain the level of definition or commitment needed to move beyond Stage Two.

Transition from the first stage to the second may also become blurred, at least for a time, because it isn't clear to the people involved what choices have or have not been made. In order to move the change effort forward, Stage Two must provide enough form and substance to the objectives and means of the change project. The effectiveness of the goals and plans of Stage Two lies in large part in their ability to stimulate interest and appropriate action within the organization beyond the Stage Two planners. Spreading commitment to others, thereby increasing the critical mass driving the change process, is an objective of Stage Three.

Stage Three: Initiating Action

If your project does gain sufficient definition and commitment, it may enter Stage Three, "Initiating Action". From Stage Two throughout the rest of the Change Cycle, you'll notice that I emphasize the need for a multi-person effort within the organizational framework. Individual expertise and commitment in driving any project is vital to its success. However, the dominant activity during this stage is to extend and exercise the organization's collective capability toward achieving your project goals.

This implies that the individuals involved agree on the value of the project, on its goals, and on how they'll go about achieving those goals. Each person must go through his or her own process to reach alignment on each of these points. Your project as an organizational endeavor may have reached the third stage of the Change Cycle, but individuals who are brought into the project now will need time to move through their own Stages One and Two. They will need to integrate the project within their work lives and commit enough energy and talent to the effort to move it forward.

Organizations have several familiar methods for securing the commitment of individuals to high-priority projects. Jobs can be restructured around the project or around the change itself. People can be evaluated for salary and promotion based on the progress of a project. If a person's income and career are tied to a venture's success, he or she will make a higher level of commitment.

But often organizations miss a fundamental step in gaining wide participant commitment: people need to understand why the work is considered important and how it fits into the larger picture of organizational goals, objectives, and long-range plans. Understanding the importance and context of a project often makes the difference between half-hearted and fully committed individuals. Answering the question "why do it?" for your participants, and wrestling with the issues that concern them, gains that extra degree of commitment.

Let's assume you have people's commitment and that the actual implementation process is underway. At this point it is vital to provide everyone with feedback on progress and results on a frequent, ongoing basis. Tangible signs of progress and better results will nourish commitment and sustain momentum. Even if the signs of progress are subtle and inconclusive at first, people need all the legitimate proof of progress they can get.

Without these signs of progress, the team will have difficulty holding the project together over time. Many projects fail because key people, including interested parties outside the core group, can't see proof of progress. Participants can become so focused on specific tasks that they lose sight of overall movement.

Even if your project is moving forward, lack of feedback from a broader perspective to team members, participants, and others who have a stake in the project can kill an effort at any point. Stakeholders can include interested officials, upper management not participating in implementing the change, shareholders, and special interest groups. This isn't simply a matter of protocol. Regular measurement of progress is critical to all who've committed to and invested themselves in the project. Keeping skeptics informed of your project's movement is also a good strategy for lessening the chance that they'll become active blockers.

As your project moves through the third stage, those involved are making changes, testing and revising procedures, and reporting results. In-progress audits assure that learning is taking place. The information gained allows you to evaluate mistakes in time to make adjustments to improve performance. Your initial goals and plans may need to be revisited and modified as more is learned during this stage. This should be relatively easy to do, because the team and its sponsors are committed, as are most of those directly responsible for implementing the change.

The work of Stage Three sometimes includes further development of plans initiated during the previous two stages. But most often it is dominated by the implementation of plans essentially completed during Stage Two. Plans need to be continually monitored and revised, sometimes well into Stage Five. But plans should be completed for all practical purposes no later than the early part of the third stage. Stage Three requires an unmistakable shift from planning to action. The organization must begin testing its ability to actually make the change happen.

By the end of Stage Three, many if not all of those who'll be making the change are probably involved. They likely view the change effort as a new factor in their work lives. Although the outcome may still be in question, they have no doubt that the change effort is real and will involve them for a significant period of time. As a result, there's no avoiding the need to form some sort of opinion and a stance toward this change process. Most participants, by the end of Stage Three, will have decided to go along with your change, at least as far as they perceive is necessary. Whether or not they believe that it is the right thing to do or worth the effort, most of them will support the implementation effort to some extent.

Stage Four: Making Connections

The real work of the change process involves achieving lasting shifts in attitude and behavior. While these shifts may begin to happen in Stage Three, this becomes a critical objective in Stage Four. In order for attitudes and behavior to truly shift, people must wrestle with the change as it plays out in their daily work. They must determine precisely which of their priorities, skills, and actions must be modified. Some will be exploring just how much actual change is necessary, and how much leeway exists for a superficial show of change.

In any case, before they can be expected to make lasting changes, people need to discuss it thoroughly and repeatedly. People also need to experience how it feels to do things in the new way. They're often comparing old and new ways of working, trying to figure out just how the new ways can fit. They're talking with others who share their situation, formulating and reformulating their ideas, looking for support, guidance, solutions to usage problems, and practical suggestions from any credible source. All of this constitutes the work of Stage Four.

As an organizational change effort moves into the fourth stage, the level of interaction about the change increases noticeably. People are not only discussing the change itself, but are also making connections between the change and all other facets of their work lives: how they do their jobs, how they think about themselves and their jobs, how they relate to others within their work units, and how they interact with other parts of the organization.

This is a time of excitement mixed with some uneasiness. Progress should be more evident by now, but the practical problems of making the change work haven't been totally solved. During this period, resistance can be strong until workable solutions to these problems are found. However, the urge to find solutions will also be strong if the participants have been brought through the earlier stages of the Change Cycle successfully. When this is the case, a palpable sense of excitement and anticipation— perhaps even adventure—is in the air as people strive to make the changes work.

Once the changes begin to take hold, those involved may feel accomplishment, pride, and personal satisfaction. For more and more people, the change is seen not as *your* change, but as *our* change. This sense of accomplishment can be strengthened if results of the change process are being measured and shared. Again, proof that the change is having the desired impact is important to virtually everyone now, and may be absolutely critical in shifting the opinions of those holdouts who have continued to doubt the potential of the change.

In Stage Four, "Making Connections", the importance of communication both within the group actually making the change and with the rest of the organization can't be overstated. This activity goes beyond merely keeping people informed. Any important change in one part of your organization will very likely lead to shifts in related parts. Interactive patterns are almost certain to be affected. Organizational roles or areas of responsibility may shift. The importance of one unit may increase, while that of another may decrease.

This daisy chain of shifts needs attention just as much as the core set of changes. In some instances, the implications or by-products of peripheral change may ultimately have more impact than the core change itself. Expect these auxiliary changes, and process them with those likely to be affected in the same way that you do the core change.

Be prepared that the fourth stage of the Change Cycle usually doesn't occur as quickly or surely as we'd like. We're often surprised just how long it takes for people—including ourselves—

to make even simple behavioral change, much less to make changes requiring the acquisition of new skills and techniques. Changes that require a shift in values, attitudes, or basic orientation require even more complex implementation processes, and these usually take much longer to accomplish. What appears straightforward in the planning stages may be much harder to implement than anyone expects.

A word of caution is appropriate. Expect some struggle even with the simplest and most compelling changes. If the potential impact of the change is significant, there will almost certainly be difficulties to overcome. Overly optimistic timetables gloss over such realities. While they may improve your early chances for getting the commitment you need to proceed, in the long run, unrealistic schedules for change can frustrate all involved. In fact, they can make it appear that a perfectly successful change effort is failing, because things are evolving more slowly than planned. Build in time for overcoming difficulties. It takes time for people to change their attitudes and behaviors. Anticipate whatever barriers you can, and then add time for unanticipated problems, as well.

By the end of Stage Four, your changes have become operational. New patterns of action are apparent, and you probably have some measurable results. You can expect that the results will continue to improve, at least through Stage Five. But the change isn't yet irreversible. The entire work system needs rebalancing before the change is a part of the natural, ongoing flow of activity.

Stage Five: Rebalancing to Accommodate the Change

As mentioned above, significant change is likely to have an impact on parts of your organization that aren't directly involved in the change effort. Adjustments will be needed throughout the system. Until that happens, an inner tension will be present in the organization as a by-product of the core change. The process of making these adjustments wherever needed is the central activity of the fifth stage, "Rebalancing". Rebalancing may be needed in functional systems, relationship patterns, and hierarchical structures of the organization. Rebalancing may be needed on a personal level, as well.

Note this does not indicate that communications to other parts of the organization should begin in Stage Five. On the contrary, all parts of the organization should be included in the communication process throughout the cycle. It means that the communications with and involvement of other affected parts of the organization takes on greater focus and emphasis during Stage Five. One reason for this is that some of the adjustments needed throughout the organization do not become clear until the primary change effort is well underway. The implications for other parts of the organization often do not crystallize until the change can be observed in action. But when it does become clear that another part of the organization must also undergo change, they understandably become much more interested and involved.

As Stage Five proceeds, there's a growing sense of balance as the pieces of the project come into alignment. But the status of the change remains precarious; it isn't fully integrated. The new patterns of work may not feel natural yet. Perhaps they don't quite fit with other aspects of the job or people's lives. During this time, tension or outright conflict can develop with other departments or associated work units who must make their own shifts to accommodate the core change.

The work of change leaders during Stage Five is to bring the entire work system to a new state of internal balance, where all the pieces function together as an integrated whole. More attention may be needed to help people complete shifts in thinking, attitudes, or behaviors before a new balance can be achieved. If problems are ignored or aren't resolved during Stage Five, it won't take much of a disruptive force to overturn the fragile change. The old way of doing things is likely to be more comfortable for people than the new way, until the rebalancing is complete.

By the end of Stage Five, the change has become the norm. People are not only comfortable with the change, but would resist going back to old patterns. If an outsider took a fresh look at the organization, it would be difficult to recognize that a change had actually occurred, because it is so much a part of the way people think about and do their work. Traces of the old ways of doing things would be hard to discover, unless you knew just where to look. The change has now stabilized, and will tend to stay in place unless disrupted by strong forces.

Stage Six: Consolidating the Learning

Once the new balance has been achieved within the groups most affected by the change, the process enters its sixth stage. This is a time to examine the change effort from a slightly different perspective. You now stand on higher ground: you can look backward on past accomplishments and forward to future possibilities.

This is a time for integration and reflection on the project as a whole and on the change itself.

◆   Were your initial goals achieved?
◆   If all of them were not achieved, how much progress did you make?
◆   What have you learned about directing change that you can apply to other initiatives?
◆   What worked and what didn't work in your change effort?
◆   What should your organization do differently the next time?
◆   What new capabilities does your organization now have as a result of the change process it has just gone through?
◆   How can your organization use those new capabilities to make further improvements?
◆   What possibilities now exist to take advantage of what has been learned?

The work of this stage is not simply to reiterate what you have already accomplished. It is also a time to look forward; seeds are planted for the future. New possibilities are identified that can spring to life as a new Change Cycle. Based on newly developed skills, systems, attitudes, and confidence in their own capability, people are likely to look forward to fresh opportunities ahead. They can think of ways to leverage both the new system and their individual and collective capability. For example, suppose your organization has worked hard to develop several key customer relationships during the current Change Cycle. Next you may be able to build on those improved customer relationships by directing a new market penetration effort at those accounts.

Stage Six is the period when all significant knowledge and learning associated with the project is integrated. As with the earlier stages, your organization may not go through this integration process at all, or may not complete it. This is always a matter of desire and choice. But if the value of this integrative step is clear to you, then your organization can use Stage Six to help guide its own evolution.

Stage Six is important because it is the natural place to simultaneously consider both past and future. It is an especially powerful moment because past accomplishments are still fresh, and the future is still open to shape as you choose. Stage Six can be viewed as a balancing point between past and future. If you emphasize only the past, you are less likely to seize upon new possibilities and move into a new cycle of change. If you jump into the future without thoroughly understanding the learnings of the past, you will likely miss the chance to leverage what you have already gained.

Stage Seven: Moving to the Next Cycle

Once integration is complete, the Change Cycle enters and quickly moves through the seventh stage, "Moving to the Next Cycle". This stage marks the point in time when one cycle reaches completion and a new cycle may begin. It is hard to imagine the successful completion of one significant change without seeds being present for another change. In order to move to a new cycle, there must be a simultaneous emphasis on what has just been completed, and what comes next.

During Stage Seven, a momentum must exist that propels the organization forward into the new cycle of change. There needs to be a clear recognition of the challenges and opportunities that lie ahead. The best possibilities for future change should already be identified and discussed to build interest and excitement. Otherwise, the transition to a new cycle may be delayed indefinitely, or may never occur. Stage Seven represents a moment when the accomplishments of the past and the potential of the future are both present. Accomplishments of the current cycle become crystallized in people's minds and attention shifts to future possibilities.

The Role of Chaos

Throughout the seven stages of the Change Cycle, resistance to change is encountered in many and varied forms. Resistance is a part of any organizational change effort, from inertia at the beginning of the process, to political opposition, to implementation complexities, to technological shortcomings, to entrenched attitudes and behavior patterns, to competitive activity, to industry-wide pressures, to macroeconomic factors. This resistance can be thought of as a force which must be overcome in order for change to occur. The force which resists change, in all its many forms, can be called Chaos. Any time the force of Chaos is encountered, progress of the Change Cycle is challenged. In order for the change to keep moving, leaders and other participants in the process must solve the problems which impede their progress. The driving force of leadership and other committed people push-ing against the resisting force of Chaos forms the most fundamental dynamic process in any organizational change effort.

A Few Points to Remember

Let me re-emphasize a few key points to remember while applying the concepts of the Change Cycle.
1. It is easier to develop good plans than to develop the organizational will to carry out those plans. Many projects— even worthwhile ones—hardly get off the ground or get bogged down in the first two stages for lack of adequate definition and support. Other change efforts fail to survive the third stage for lack of aligned collective effort.
2. When a project does manage to get to the fourth stage, it's often prematurely considered "complete". Active management of the project may end at this point, or too soon after

the initial problems of implementation are resolved. That not only shortchanges the effort needed to sustain the change during Stage Four, but leaves the remaining stages subject to problems arising from lack of definition, undermanagement, or total neglect. The Change Cycle then may never be completed, regardless of how well managed and successful the first three stages have been.

3. Stage Five is just as important. This is the stage during which integration into the organization takes place, and the organization begins to enjoy the desired results and beneficial by-products. If Stage Five is neglected, the likelihood that the change will take hold is dramatically decreased. If the change does not become the norm, it is likely to unravel over time.

4. The integration of learning in Stage Six assures that you will gain not only from the change itself, but from all that has been learned from the process of making the change. If this work is skipped, the organization will not fully understand what has been achieved and what this can mean for the organization's future.

5. Projects and other change initiatives are often defined in terms of goals that could be technically accomplished by the end of Stage Three or sometime during Stage Four. This occurs frequently with internally managed efforts, and even more frequently when external resources such as consultants are used. Without committed managers who are conscious of the existence and importance of the final stages—mainly the fourth stage and beyond—projects fall short of their real potential and change that has occurred may not last.

At each key point of an initiative, the use of the seven-stage Change Cycle will help in clarifying your organization's issues, tasks, and roles. This model shows you the issues to be faced and defines the completion point for each stage. The purpose and value of the process is to promote understanding of the sequence of events typical of any change effort, and to minimize the inevitable surprises along the way.

As you put this model into practice, the concept of project management will take on new meaning; your whole notion of the scope and boundaries of managing projects and other change initiatives may shift radically. While this model doesn't give managers all the answers or skills needed to successfully guide change processes, I hope that it does provide you with information and guidelines that may previously have been missing or scattered, increasing your likelihood of managing change successfully.

Chart 1. Change Cycle Summary

The following chart summarizes the desired outcomes to be reached, actions to be taken, and typical barriers to overcome at each stage of the Change Cycle.

STAGE ONE: CHOOSING THE TARGET

Desired Outcomes
- A vision or other clearly expressed target
- Recognition of the positive potential of the target
- An individual or a leadership group strongly believes in the target
- Forward momentum

Actions
- Identify possibilities and opportunities
- Select the best ones
- Gain sufficient commitment to begin the process
- Set a target or general direction of effort
- Create a description of a future state (vision) in which the target has been achieved

Issues and Barriers to Overcome
- Not having enough reason to change—not enough pain, opportunity, or recognized potential
- Rejecting new ideas prematurely, before they are fairly evaluated
- Not gaining an initial commitment

STAGE TWO: SETTING GOALS

Desired Outcomes

- Specific goals
- Action plans
- Organizational commitment to provide enough resources to get the job done
- Clarified vision based on better understanding of what success will look like
- Growing number of people who support the change (number may still be small)

Actions

- Test the feasibility of making the change
- Envision what success looks like with greater detail and precision than in Stage One
- Develop specific goals and action plans needed to reach the target
- Develop a clear understanding of resource requirements, skills and tools needed, timing, and practical hurdles
- Gain a substantial commitment to the time and resources required

Issues and Barriers to Overcome

- Not having a deep enough commitment based on practical requirements once the goals, plans, and hurdles are clear
- Having an insufficient focus on the change, too many other priorities

STAGE THREE: INITIATING ACTION

Desired Outcomes ————————————————————————
- Greater confidence: the organization has proven to itself that there is enough capability present to make the change
- Substantial increase in ownership and participation in the change
- Some tangible evidence of movement toward the goal
- The changes are operative throughout the chosen arena (or at least throughout a large portion of the chosen arena)
- Critical mass of support for the change has begun to gel
- Good progress toward resolving start-up problems is evident

Actions ————————————————————————
- Begin to carry out the plan
- Involve all those who must change: explain why as well as what and how
- Many people are actually making shifts in the way they do work
- Exercise individual and group capability toward goals.
- Demonstrate effectiveness of the plan and progress toward goals
- Measure and report tangible proof of the benefits of the change as soon as possible

Issues and Barriers to Overcome ————————————————————————
- Not having the proper resources to overcome the known practical implementation hurdles
- Underestimating the time, effort, and expectations required to bring each new participant on board
- Lacking the necessary skills and tools needed to do the job well
- Not identifying implementation problems as they crop up and not resolving them effectively

STAGE FOUR: MAKING CONNECTIONS

Desired Outcomes _____

- Start-up problems are resolved
- Most people who are expected to make the change have done so
- Ownership in the change is widespread
- Improved functioning and results are more apparent than in Stage Three
- The change has actually been demonstrated throughout the chosen arena
- The changes are not only operating, but are beginning to work smoothly and effectively

Actions _____

- Complete the practical translation of the change in terms of how it affects the way work is done
- Encourage and support everyone as they grapple with how the change will play out in their work: what precisely will change and what will remain the same—tasks, procedures, interfaces, priorities
- Talk about, think about, and try out new ways of doing things
- Improve the new approach based on usage and feedback

Issues and Barriers to Overcome _____

- Limiting or trying to short-cut the personal interaction needed to firmly plant the change
- Not allowing each new participant to build his or her own buy-in, by personally going through Stages One, Two, and Three, before initiating Stage Four
- Leaders and other active sponsors shift their focus to other matters too soon, before change is irreversible

STAGE FIVE: REBALANCING TO ACCOMMODATE THE CHANGE

Desired Outcomes _____

◆ Improved results and benefits are clear and persuasive
◆ Stability of the change is relatively complete throughout the entire work arena
◆ A new balance has been established throughout the organization
◆ The changes have become the norm; it would be difficult at the end of this stage to reverse them

Actions _____

◆ Identify the ripple effects of the change: how does it affect other departments, functions, or layers of the hierarchy? What are the implications for current systems and organizational structure? How does it affect key interfaces (customers, suppliers, constituents, other agencies...)?
◆ Integrate the changes throughout the entire work arena to blend with existing attitudes, systems, and ways of doing work

Issues and Barriers to Overcome _____

◆ Change not stabilized yet; regression is still possible
◆ Resistance to change emerges in other parts of the organization, as they have to make adjustments
◆ Assuming the change process is complete before this rebalancing has occurred

STAGE SIX: CONSOLIDATING THE LEARNING

Desired Outcomes
- The extent and limits of the change are understood
- Lessons learned are now ready to be applied to further Change Cycles
- New possibilities and potential have been identified
- People are beginning to look forward to what comes next

Actions
- Audit accomplishments against original goals and plans
- Identify what worked, what didn't, and why
- Celebrate accomplishments; share learnings
- Assess which aspects of the original target have been realized and which have not
- Identify the new possibilities and potential that exist now as a result of what has been achieved
- Start thinking and talking about what comes next

Issues and Barriers to Overcome
- Not recognizing the value of a formal reflective process
- Not consolidating learnings, creating a barrier to the next Change Cycle—failing to identify new potential
- Attending only to past accomplishments and shortcomings—not identifying future possibilities

STAGE SEVEN: MOVING TO THE NEXT CYCLE

Desired Outcomes _____

- People have a sense of completion and a readiness to move on to the next challenge
- People recognize the need for further change and are beginning to get excited about the new possibilities
- Momentum has been built, leading to the next Change Cycle

Actions _____

- Complete reflections on the old cycle
- Feel a sense of satisfaction and completion in what has been accomplished
- Recognize the need and potential that lie immediately ahead
- Continue to discuss the best new possibilities for the future; during these discussions, express the clear intent to move immediately ahead into the next Change Cycle

Issues and Barriers to Overcome _____

- Not recognizing this stage as a transition point rather than an end point
- Selling short your ability to make further significant changes

Chart 2. Patterns Within the Change Cycle

Each Change Cycle is unique, with its own identifiable character and dynamics. For this reason, it is not possible to state unequivocally which activities take place in which stage. I have identified the typical sequence and pattern of activities, issues, and outcomes throughout the seven stages of the Change Cycle. This information is designed to be used as a general guide, not as an inviolable template to be imposed upon your change effort.

There are also typical trends in activities and key factors that cut across the boundaries between stages. It is useful to monitor these as the Change Cycle unfolds. The chart below summarizes these major trends.

Keep in mind that although the stages in the Change Cycle have been presented in a sequential manner, in practice there is fluidity and blending of certain activities and objectives between the stages. This is shown on the chart by the carryover of activity from one stage to another.

There is certainly dovetailing and overlap between stages. Activities, barriers, and desired outcomes can coincide. Note on chart 2 that certain processes such as planning, the building of commitment, and implementation take several stages to complete. Note also that planning does not entirely stop when implementing begins. Planning and implementing overlap, but the balance between these activities shifts predictably throughout the cycle. Other examples of overlap can be found by examining the Change Cycle Summary (Chart 1) immediately preceding this discussion. This overlap does not mean it is hard to tell which stage you are in. The dominant activities, barriers, and goals will shift in a predictable sequence as you move through a change cycle, despite any overlap.

It usually takes quite a while before any solid evidence of results is tangible. Whether you are looking for evidence of the anticipated benefits of the change, or for evidence that the change will become permanent and irreversible, you will probably have

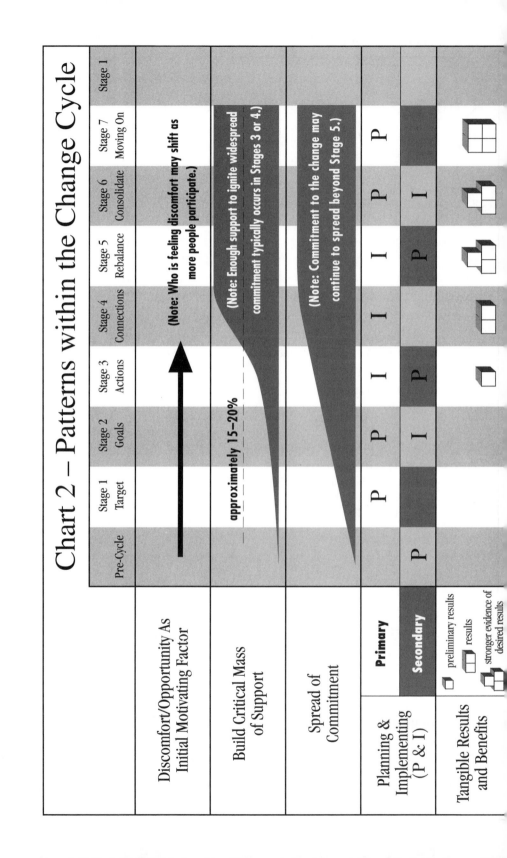

Chart 2 – Patterns within the Change Cycle

	Pre-Cycle	Stage 1 Target	Stage 2 Goals	Stage 3 Actions	Stage 4 Connections	Stage 5 Rebalance	Stage 6 Consolidate	Stage 7 Moving On	Stage 1
Dominant Time Orientation (Past, Present, Future)	Present (painful stimulus)	Future	Future	Present	Present	Present	Past and Future (reflections)	Present (reflections) Future (What's next?)	
Typical Shifts in Ownership		Shift to leader	Shift to core team	Shift to participants	Shift to more participants	Shift to other areas within organization			
Change Becomes Stable/Irreversable							✓		
Resistance to Change	✓	✓	✓	✓	✓	✓	✓ (resistance to next cycle begins)	✓	

to wait much longer than you find comfortable. Even if preliminary indications of benefits appear in Stage Three, you will most likely want more solid proof of results before being convinced that your change effort is succeeding. These solid indications may not occur until well into Stage Five, and the change will not stabilize fully until the end of Stage Five. The caution here is patience. It takes people a long time and a great deal of discussion, independent thought, formulation, trial, reformulation, and retrial to assimilate a significant organizational change. The kind of communication required spans the entire Change Cycle, and cannot be rushed. Leaders are in the difficult position of putting themselves on the line to achieve a desired change, yet having to wait much longer than they want or usually anticipate for substantive results. During the long period of uncertainty the pressure for proof builds, sometimes on a daily basis. Pressure can come from superiors within the organization, from outside sources such as competitive activity, or from the participants in the change process themselves. There is little that can be done to leapfrog the step-by-step process of change, or the assimilation time that people require. Leaders must simply prepare themselves to deal with the wait and with the pressures they will certainly have to face.

One of the patterns identified in Chart 2 refers to the dominant time orientation within each stage. The dominant time orientation is linked to the primary objectives and activities of each stage. For example, in Stage Six, a primary activity is to examine what has been accomplished to date in the change effort, and to look at implications for the future. So the time orientation is described as "past and future." Identifying the dominant time orientation can be useful in determining when you have actually shifted to another stage. Movement from Stage Two to Stage Three, for example, usually means a shift in focus from planning future implementation to carrying out those plans. There is a shift from a future to a present orientation.

Commitment Versus Critical Mass

Let me try to clarify two closely related trends shown on Chart 2: the spread of commitment and the development of a critical mass of support. Commitment is defined here as willing support of the change effort. Critical mass is defined as the number of committed people needed to ignite the spread of commitment throughout a larger group of people.

It is fascinating to watch commitment to a change build within a group. At first, only a few people may want to change. It may take quite a while before this number increases significantly. But there is a point within the cycle where the desire for the change seems to ignite and spread rapidly throughout the group. This point is reached when a critical mass of people actively support a change. My observation is that critical mass is reached when about fifteen to twenty percent of the people directly involved with a change are truly committed. This level of commitment may occur during Stage Three, or may not occur until well into Stage Four. The number of people who are committed to the change—who willingly support it—continues to grow through Stage Five and perhaps beyond.

Chapter 2

An Example of the Change Cycle: Modernizing a Factory

The seven stages of the Change Cycle seem to take a straightforward pathway in principle. But what happens when you apply these ideas to live situations? How does the Change Cycle evolve in practice? How do you recognize where in a cycle of change your organization is? What are the objectives and typical activities in each stage? What kinds of problems can you expect to face as you plan and implement change?

Let's look in on a major change effort in a troubled fictional company, Cunningham Aviation. I'll identify each stage of the Change Cycle as you follow Cunningham's story. After each stage, I'll briefly review what has happened and its significance in the change process.

Reviving Cunningham Aviation

Cunningham is the General Motors of aviation instruments, a venerable pioneer company whose name is synonymous with all-American quality and reliability. In recent years, however, Cunningham's management has perpetuated a near-fatal error in judgment: they've ignored signs of restlessness in their long-time customer base. Even confronted by declining sales and a few outright defections, they continued to believe they were invincible in the marketplace.

Cunningham's complacency recently caught up with them. In the course of ten months, two relative newcomers to the industry lured away thirteen percent of their business base. As Cunningham's management considered how to interpret this news, several other major contracts were nearing renewal dates. The word from marketing? Not one of these customers was talking convincingly about its future with Cunningham.

Cunningham conceded to calling the customer migration a trend. But what was wrong? And more important, how could they fix it? Management contracted with a consultant to troubleshoot the situation. Two months and another lost customer later, the consultant had uncovered several critical problem areas.

♦ Cunningham was overly reliant on its reputation and historical dominance, and was correspondingly slow to respond to contemporary opportunities and customer needs.

♦ The product line was of consistently high quality but, technologically, it was out-of-date by at least six years.

♦ Cunningham had grown organizationally top-heavy. New ideas from outside the elite management group rarely were heard or acted upon.

♦ Cunningham's plant was well maintained, but its equipment— like its product line—was out-of-date, and the manufacturing processes were labor-intensive.

And there was more. His conclusions supported by overwhelming evidence, the consultant reported the bottom line: Cunningham had a choice: change, or endure a painful period of attrition and eventually go out of business. Cunningham chose to change.

Stage One: Developing a New Vision for Cunningham

Cunningham had no trouble identifying its immediate objective: to regain market leadership. Management determined to move aggressively, starting first with the organization of a research and development team to design a new line of products. At the urging of the consultant, Cunningham then reluctantly agreed to hire an outsider to head the entire transition effort. They knew this would ruffle some feathers, but were convinced that the best man for the job was not at Cunningham.

Jerry Muldauer was formerly a partner in a successful newer company—one that was accounting for a good share of Cunningham's customer defections. Most people were surprised that Jerry bit at Cunningham's offer. But for Jerry, the challenge of restoring vitality to the aging giant had considerable appeal. As Cunningham's new general manager, he was given almost entrepreneurial independence and freedom to operate his division, including the final word on most manufacturing decisions. He would report directly to the CEO, and interact frequently with the board of directors.

Jerry didn't have much time for setting the transition in motion. He started by immersing himself in existing plant operations. Which systems, processes, and equipment might continue to work, with or without modification, to produce the new line? Who were the employees now in the plant, and how could their skills be adapted? For two weeks, Jerry observed and asked questions. He got acquainted with people and their strengths, and assessed the gaps in their collective skills. The workers also got to know him and were able to discuss their ideas. While evaluating the plant, Jerry was building his relationship with the work force. Part of their willingness and ability to change would depend upon their trust in his intentions and judgment.

As a result of these conversations, Jerry was filled with information and ideas. He had a pretty good grasp of how things were done in the plant, and how they could be improved. But he was not quite ready to draft his plan of action. First, he wanted some outside perspective. So he devoted the next few days to outside contacts. There were several people within the industry who could be counted on for valuable insights.

There were also key customers Jerry felt he must talk to before making any changes to the product line. If they had strong objections or limited interest, he could redirect the product development effort before it went too far in the wrong direction. The latest market research was useful, but a lot could still be gained by speaking to customers directly. Jerry believed that customers had a firm grasp of what they needed and wanted. He could use their insights to help shape Cunningham's future. Of course, it would have been better to get this customer input before the design team, which was set up before he was hired, had begun their work. However, Jerry was trying to do the best he could with the situation he had inherited. It was still early in the design process, and any redirection of the team's efforts was likely to be minor.

Jerry also wanted to soften the ground for future product introductions by making customers a part of the new product development process. What better way to make customers receptive to new products than to see their ideas incorporated in those products?

Three weeks had now passed since Jerry had joined Cunningham. He had spoken at length to employees at all levels in the organization, and to quite a few sources outside the company. It was time to formulate his plan of action. Jerry knew the aviation market well, and his greatest asset was his almost infallible sense of aviation's future. The sophisticated line of aviation instruments and guidance control equipment that the design team was working on represented a strong bridge between the present and future markets. Cunningham was committed to modernizing its plant to produce the new line. With that commitment in his back pocket, Jerry was confident that he could transform Cunningham's plant back into a world-class operation.

Jerry turned his attention next to planning for the biggest single transition effort in Cunningham's history. The company had to survive the next few years, or his long-range vision wouldn't even matter. He needed to refocus his attention not on the state of aviation five years from now, but on the current and complex problem of bringing R&D's new product line into existence.

Alone in his office, Jerry began to consider the enormous job he had taken on. On the plus side, Cunningham was willing and able to finance the plant changeover. If Jerry's modernized plant could produce quality products and keep a tight rein on costs, Cunningham's marketing and distribution departments would take care of the rest.

On the other hand, Cunningham had virtually no modern precision mass-production facilities. While the company had employed and trained a wealth of highly skilled technicians, their strength was in producing hand-tooled instruments. Could these skills be adapted to modern high-tech production? Major changes would be needed: new machinery, new systems and processes, a new skill base, and probably many new people.

Besides these difficulties, it was apparent that any change in the plant must be made while continuing to turn out the old product line. This meant some compromise in terms of keeping customers satisfied with a declining volume of older product while overhauling the product line, the factory, and their manufacturing procedures. Jerry knew that it would be quite a challenge to meet his existing business and performance measurements while making sweeping changes. He girded himself for the onslaught of pressure from his board of directors, as he prepared to make major changes while delivering the best possible profits during the transition period.

Still alone in thought, Jerry scanned through all that he had seen and heard, and reviewed reports prepared earlier by staff and the consultant. He sketched alternate physical plant layouts, imagining people at work in each one. He then selected one of the new guidance instruments being designed as a model. Jerry imagined in minute detail each stage in its manufacture. He visualized it undergoing final adjustment and testing, and moving out the door, eventually into the hands of the end user. He imagined pilots and navigators using the new instrument, considering how it changed the way they did things.

By guiding his imagination and using this method of mental testing, Jerry was able to weed out problems and develop his more productive ideas.[1] Soon he was ready to pull the best ideas together into a plan that he could share with others. He scheduled a two-hour company-wide meeting. By the end of the meeting Jerry had set the transitional effort into motion.

As he spoke of the changes to come, Jerry's confidence and enthusiasm radiated throughout the crowd. Management, staff, and technicians alike sat in rapt attention as Jerry communicated his vision. He drew word pictures of the physical plant, of the

---

[1] *This technique, called a thought experiment, is discussed on pages 154–157.*

work that people were doing, and even of how it could feel to be part of the new operation. He described teams assuming responsibility for individual products, and how the teams could, within certain bounds, develop their own systems and methods for manufacture. He painted a bright and convincing future for Cunningham, reestablishing its industry leadership.

When Jerry finished, the room fell silent. No one budged, but the energy was almost tangible. The target Jerry had described was compelling and, as he laid it out, achievable. As people began to react, talking among themselves about the changes to come, Jerry took only a moment to congratulate himself on the effectiveness of his presentation. Then he tuned in to the mood of the group. The excitement and optimism were growing, but Jerry also caught some stirrings of anxiety. He felt it as well. Even if everyone believed the plant modernization was essential and achievable, the task ahead was still monumental, requiring a great deal of change on everyone's part.

Discussion

The first stage of the Change Cycle is dedicated to giving definition to the specific change. Stage One, "Choosing the Target", is characterized by an open-minded attitude toward new possibilities, novel approaches to recurring problems, and testing of alternatives. Without this receptivity to potential opportunities, no Change Cycle could begin. But where does this receptivity come from?

Receptivity often results from the recognition of a critical problem or a compelling opportunity. In order to address the problem or to take advantage of the opportunity, ideas must be generated and evaluated. In practice, people are frequently pushed into change by unpleasant, often painful circumstances. More often than not, though they may see the need to change, they don't want to make the effort. The initial motivation often comes from external events, as it did in Cunningham's case. Shifts in the industry, the economy, technology, one's customer base, available resources, competitors, and so forth can force the need to change.

Once sufficient need or opportunity for change is clearly recognized, the stage is set to begin a Change Cycle. At the beginning, acknowledgment of the need for change may be tentative or reluctant, but this can develop into a strong desire as the Change Cycle moves along. Remember that the desire for change need not be intense at the outset. You will have plenty of opportunity to test whether the targeted change is worth doing, and to build commitment throughout the first few stages of the process.

In the first stage of any Change Cycle, you identify and evaluate many possibilities. Each option must be examined sufficiently to judge its potential value to the organization, as well as its fit and feasibility. A selection process takes place. Once a single option has risen above the others, that option must be developed into a fairly clear organizational target, one that can be communicated and understood.

The target can be firmed up in many ways. One method is to formulate a vision statement that describes how things will be once the change is made. In order to formulate such a statement about the future, you will probably need to refine your original idea several times. By the time a clear target has been identified, at least one person believes in it. And before the first stage of the Change Cycle is complete, several other people in the organization may be as committed to the target as you.

However, personal commitment isn't enough. In practice, most major change efforts require a formal commitment from the organization's leadership to provide adequate resources to carry out the change process. If the selected target isn't important or compelling enough to gain such commitment, the Change Cycle will simply stall here.

In our example, Jerry was hired to respond to external market forces and to an internal corporate mandate, both of which were driving the need for this change. Jerry recognized that he first needed to choose his own target—to gather enough data to test the potential of alternative ideas. He didn't expect to complete a detailed and well-analyzed plan in the short time available for this stage. But he could, and did, push himself to make calculated guesses. He knew he could tackle any unanswered questions in more depth in the coming weeks. Once his thoughts were crystallized and his own excitement built, then he described his vision to others in a way that spread the excitement.

Stage Two: Planning for the Transition

Jerry was pleased that his vision-sharing meeting had gone well. With a few of his own staff, he developed a master coordinating plan. It set overall goals for the plant and identified milestones, methods for measuring progress, and feedback mechanisms. Next Jerry organized planning teams for each phase of the transition: equipment acquisition and setup, human resources assessment, worker training, better linkage between product engineering and the manufacturing process, and so on. Each team's activities were coordinated to be consistent with the master plan.

Now the plant buzzed with excitement. The grapevine had never borne quite so many rumors, despite Jerry's efforts to keep everyone current. Whatever people didn't know, they imagined; their speculations were mostly negative. Would there be layoffs? Who'd be reassigned to new tasks? Could the product team concept work here? Did Jerry intend to be with Cunningham long-term, or would he leave as soon as the changes were made and he got a better offer? Although the path to change became clearer as the planning team's work progressed, uneasiness persisted throughout the plant.

Jerry attacked the negative rumors and associated worries head on with more frequent updates. As plans began to take shape, they were immediately shared with the work force. This helped everyone become increasingly clear about their new goals and the action steps needed for reaching them. Unease gradually gave way to relief, as the majority of the workers began preparing for the actual work of making the changes happen. For many, this was an important time—the moment when their desire to make the changes came into sharp focus.

Still others remained skeptical. They'd never had to make such huge changes in the way they performed their jobs. But while these employees still had unanswered questions and worries, they acknowledged that this change was the only known path to corporate survival. So even these reluctant workers had excellent reasons for throwing themselves into the change process, despite their doubts and fears. There was also a small group which was very comfortable with the old way of doing things. They could be counted on to resist any change, regardless of its merits, and were not yet showing any signs of accepting the change effort.

As Jerry tried to persuade the work force that his plan was a good one, there were opposing forces at work. Tim Bradley was Jerry's strongest manager, but he was now finding ways to undermine Jerry's efforts. He had been a contender for Jerry's position, but lost the job to Jerry. Tim played the role of the loyal opposition. There was little doubt that he would go along with the proposed change effort in the long run, but for now Tim was asking all the difficult questions. He was bringing up the right questions, but at the wrong times. Instead of voicing his concerns privately to Jerry, Tim chose moments when he put Jerry on the spot.

His manner of "sincere concern" did not hide his resentment of Jerry. Tim seemed blindly determined to show everyone that he was the better man by pointing out potential flaws in Jerry's approach. Worse still, Tim's continual jabs in the name of thorough analysis had begun to aggravate Jerry. Every time he said something in an open forum, Jerry would automatically turn his eyes to Tim, awaiting the opposing response. Jerry was trying to hold his temper, but knew it was just a matter of time before he would let his anger show. It was not a face he wished to exhibit to his employees.

Jerry also realized that if Tim remained unchecked, he could undermine the change effort before it got rolling. At this early stage of the process there was plenty of inertia to overcome without this public display of opposition. Jerry decided that he had to defuse Tim's impact, and came up with a plan.

He would first sit down with Tim in private and talk through all of Tim's concerns about the proposed changes. This would be handled as a means of getting Tim's best constructive input for the project. A week later, Tim would be given a vital assignment requiring a great deal of travel. This assignment would keep him away from the office. Tim would become a high-level advance man for the new product line. For the next several months, he would visit Cunningham's most important customers to let them know personally about the new product line. He would also explain the manufacturing innovations being made, and how these innovations would produce even higher-quality products at competitive prices. By putting Tim into a role where he had to convince others of the value of the new product line and manufacturing techniques, he would probably align himself to the change effort. There was little chance of Tim saying anything to hurt the effort, since he would be hurting himself at the same time. Moreover, this was a role that Tim would probably relish, because of the exposure to high-level managers and the chance to display his considerable persuasive powers.

Jerry gave a sigh of relief as he thought about this plan. With Tim's opposition muted, Jerry could focus his attention on building forward momentum in the organization. This included working specifically with other employees who resisted the new plans, as well as the work force in general to build commitment and enthusiasm for the change effort.

After a time, Jerry stepped back to assess progress. The level of support for their new strategy was growing. He was encouraged to see that as the planning teams were able to set firm goals for the transition, nearly everyone understood and was at least somewhat motivated to achieve them.

Discussion

Stage Two, "Setting Goals", is characterized by its emphasis on planning. Typically, more people are involved in Stage Two than in Stage One. Through this planning effort, goals become more precisely defined and practical action plans are developed. The degree and kind of effort needed to make the proposed change becomes increasingly apparent to those involved.

Ideas are tested for feasibility during this period. This testing can take many forms: critical analysis within the planning team, rigorous costing out of the change, discussions with workers who must make changes in their work procedures, discussions with suppliers and customers, perhaps a pilot test or computer simulation. Planners may call on all the knowledge, expertise, and relevant experience that is available, either within or outside the primary planning group.

Many change efforts never pass this testing. Despite commitments from the organization's leadership and the belief of those who've gotten the process started, commitment from most others involved will be based largely on their finding value in the change. If people can't find sufficient worth in the proposed change, if they can't believe that the change is feasible, the effort will be much harder (but not impossible!) to keep moving.

In any Change Cycle, people typically ask these same questions: Is the change feasible for my organization, at this time? How do you translate a concept about what the future could be like into an operational plan? How do you stage the effort? Do I actually believe this is the right thing to do, or am I just going along with it because it's my job? If the proposed change survives this testing, the result will be a larger number of people committed to it.

Stage Two, "Setting Goals", is critical not only because of its products—the plans and goals that are developed—but because the organization's will or desire to make the required changes becomes focused during this stage. At first, only a few people at Cunningham believed in the necessity for change. These few may have thought from the outset that the change was absolutely vital, but others were much less committed. During Stage Two, more people became involved, and their commitment grew accordingly. Not only did they participate in the planning process, but they wrestled with fundamental questions regarding the change.

As is true in most businesses, Jerry didn't have the luxury of halting manufacture of the current products while switching to the new line of instruments. Careful planning was needed as Jerry had to introduce substantial changes in their manufacturing process while continuing to meet existing business goals. He had to find a way to make these major changes without creating too much disruption in the flow of the older product line.

Most significant changes in both business and governmental settings must be made while the organization continues to meet its existing objectives. Frequently, organizational commitment is compromised when it becomes obvious that some disruption is necessary in order to accomplish important change. It is unrealistic to expect to make significant change without at least some disruption. This disruption is part of the cost of making the change; it is part of the investment that must be made to achieve the benefits of the change.

Stage Three: Initiating Changes in the Plant

The time had come to act; full-scale roll out of the change was now underway. Although reduced manufacture of the older product line continued, almost everyone seemed to be busy with some aspect of the transition: choosing new equipment, revising floor plans, working out the physical logistics of moving out old equipment and bringing in new, thinking through an entirely different work flow, and coordinating with design engineers to assure producible drawings.

A difficult juggling act had now begun: manufacture of the older products had to somehow continue with as little disturbance as possible, while extensive changes were implemented. Many people shook their heads as the work day got longer and complications began to pile up. But there was also a firm determination among the work force. They knew this was the right thing to do, and many rose to the challenge.

Eventually, the day for changing out the plant equipment arrived. With new machines in place and work spaces set up, many assumed that the hardest part of the transition was over. So as everyone milled around examining the new machinery, Jerry called for quiet so he could set the stage for what would happen next.

"This is a moment to remember... a new beginning for Cunningham, for us all. Without all that you've done in the past, every one of you, we wouldn't be here right now. Without your recent support and hard work, there wouldn't be a future for Cunningham. I know you're tired, you've worked long and hard to get us to this day, and you deserve a break. But I have to tell you that the real work of changing this plant has just begun.

"We're all going to be learning a lot of new things—how to run the new machinery, how to work together as product teams, how to blend the manual technology this company grew up on with the latest manufacturing techniques. We'll need to use every bit of our capability to meet these challenges. You'll be spending a lot of your time figuring out just how to make this new system work. None of us can do it alone—but we can do it together!"

Discussion

In large organizations, a relatively small number of people are involved in the first and second stages of the Change Cycle. It isn't necessary for everyone to roll up their sleeves and spend a large part of the work day developing plans or doing preliminary feasibility testing. Typically, the number of people actively involved in the change effort increases significantly during Stage Three, "Initiating Action."

Now is the time for implementation. Now is the time when the organization as a whole (or at least the area where the change is being made) begins using all of its collective capability to make the changes that have been thought about, talked about, and planned for.

Stage Three, "Initiating Action", is the period when doing begins to take precedence over planning. Planning doesn't necessarily stop altogether, but there is a noticeable shift in emphasis. There is also a shift in the sheer activity level in the organization. Many people are now involved, setting different aspects of the change process into motion. An atmosphere of excitement builds as you progress with implementing changes. Remember that preceding this burst of activity was a period of waiting, anticipation, and uncertainty typical of Stage Two, "Setting Goals." Once in Stage Three, "Initiating Action", finally knowing what to do and taking action brings relief from the waiting period.

During Stage Three, the capability of the organization is exercised to overcome many forms of implementation problems.

The key question to be answered during this stage is "Do we have enough skills, expertise, and practical problem-solving capability to make the change work in practice?" The answer to this question is usually clear by the end of Stage Three. If there is enough capability, driven by a strong organizational commitment, resistance to the change is likely to be overcome. By the end of Stage Three, more people believe they can make the change work, even if actual results only hint at future success. It is even possible to have a ground swell of momentum building as you enter Stage Four. Let's return to Cunningham.

Stage Four: Learning a New Way of Working

New jobs, new skills, new teams, new frustrations, and always the unexpected—as Jerry warned, everyone was on a steep learning curve. Each time something a little different was tried, something unforeseen seemed to result. The optimism and motivation everyone brought to this stage in the change process was challenged daily by recurrent frustration and uncertainty.

People spent a great deal of time talking together. Some grumbled, wishing away the flux that was now so much a part of their everyday lives. But mostly, people were simply trying to come to terms with all that was happening. They discussed their new roles and relationships, the problems they encountered working as teams and their heightened sense of team accountability, and potential improvements to the new products.

Workers began solving problems as they appeared. They wrestled with their own doubts and uncertainties and assimilated new skills and viewpoints. As they learned, new products were coming off the line—at first slowly and with quality problems. Many units were scrapped during those early days. But the workers' motivation remained high. There was a constant state of interaction around these issues. The problem-solving cycle—problem occurrence, problem identification, generation of possible solutions, and testing of alternatives—was short. The feedback loop was rapid and continuous, involving many people. Improvements were quick to happen and quality products were soon being produced—slowly, but in a relatively smooth flow.

At last, Cunningham's customers were able to actually see and test the new instruments. Up until now, customers had discussed product concepts and potential features. Now the company could get customer reaction to actual products. Orders started trickling in—a favorable sign—and this early market feedback was shared with everyone in the plant. Cunningham's conviction that it could return as an industry contender was appearing well grounded. Connections were being made internally, as workers brought old and new skills to bear, participating fully in solving production problems. And the external linkages were also being reinforced, as customers tested Cunningham's new products and began placing orders.

But no change process, no matter how well conceived, is immune to unanticipated problems. For Cunningham, it came in the form of competitive activity. Advanced Aviation, Cunningham's major competitor, unexpectedly launched a new line of instruments. These instruments represented a techno-logical leap forward compared to anything currently on the market: they improved on the current leading-edge digital technology by enhanced electronic linking of the aircraft components. But it was the price that truly sent shock waves through Cunningham. Not only were these instruments techno-logically superior to Cunningham's new models, they were twenty percent lower in price. It appeared that Cunningham had fallen behind their competitors. As news of the new Advanced Aviation products reached the Cunningham work force, everyone seemed shocked and deflated. They felt that no matter how well they made their internal changes, or how good their products were, their problems were not over. In reaction to this depressing news, people began to doubt their new products and methods, and silently contemplated an uncertain future.

It was up to Jerry to counter this mood and the unspoken doubts about the company's future, but how? Jerry needed some private time to consider the situation and to plan his move. He knew the owner of an aircraft engine remanufacturing shop within a few blocks of the Cunningham plant, and arranged to disappear into one of their offices for a few hours. He could not disappear for long, without people wondering why, but he did need to get his thoughts together.

By the end of the morning Jerry had things sorted out. He was also anxious to return to his plant. There was something he had to say to his employees. As soon as he got back, he gathered everyone together for a brief message.

"You've all heard about Advanced Aviation's new instrument line, and if it's as good as we suspect, it certainly represents a challenge to our new digital products. But Advanced Aviation's new technology and cost-cutting manufacturing methods are unproven. Nobody knows how dependable and durable their instruments are. You all know that our customers demand absolute reliability; they need proof that a product will perform infallibly under real-life conditions. Too much is at stake for them to take a chance with their instrumentation. How would you weigh a few dollars' savings against the uncertainty of a new technology that just might fail when you need it the most? Our new instruments still represent the highest quality in the industry. And as we master our new production methods, we'll be able to lower our manufacturing costs, and be able to compete on price— if we have to. Also, we can wait and see how Advanced Aviation's new technology fares. If it proves to be successful, we can improve on it in our next generation of instruments. We can learn from their efforts, and go the next step. We're doing the right thing. We're building the right products the right way, and our customers are smart enough to recognize real value when they see it."

Jerry had done his best, but as he watched the workers return to their jobs, he sensed that they were not completely convinced. They still had their doubts, and those doubts could interfere with the change process. People would need to see tangible proof in the form of substantial sales of their own products before their fears would truly dissipate. Jerry could only hope that these uncertainties would not undermine the completion of their change process. He was counting on the intense activity of implementing the change as a good counter for these fears.

Discussion

Once many people are actively pursuing the change, there is a period—sometimes quite lengthy—when people are learning the new way of doing things. They are translating all the new concepts and technologies into revised patterns of action. This learning process is characterized by a great deal of interaction, to build bridges between what is new and what is already known and familiar.

The connections made during this stage are not only from person to person, but from the old ways of thinking and doing things to new ways. New skills and methods are compared, contrasted, and ultimately understood based on their similarities to and differences from older practices. In this way, continuity is always maintained between past and present. People can gain some feeling of balance and a sense of knowing how things will eventually fit together by playing out the new methods versus the old. Gradually, through this learning process, the new ways replace the old ways, both in thought and in action.

Note that there were some indications of good results occurring during Stage Four at Cunningham. The new internal process began to smooth out and orders for the new instruments started to trickle in. Tangible results are typically present during Stage Four. If all goes well, positive results and other benefits should become more apparent as the Change Cycle moves into its later stages.

Stage Five: Establishing a New Balance at Cunningham

Despite the underlying uncertainties caused by the new Advanced Aviation product line, Cunningham's internal changes were beginning to take hold. The new roles and systems were becoming comfortable, and the work force continued to refine production techniques. The balance between production of old and new products had begun to shift. More and more of the new products were being produced, while production of the older products decreased. The plant now produced quality new products at an acceptable, if unremarkable rate. Problems remained to be solved but, overall, people recognized that the system was working.

This was true for work teams, as well as for individuals. Teams functioned fairly smoothly and individuals demonstrated new areas of competence. Success stories cropped up throughout the plant: stories of people whose ideas had made an important difference and of others whose ability to smooth out difficulties added greatly to team unity. In the team environment, many employees enjoyed their work more than ever before. They could see the parts of the new manufacturing process beginning to mesh into a balanced, harmonious whole.

Jerry continued to attend to all that was happening. He saw plenty of evidence that the transition was taking hold. Many people had experienced the benefits of the new methods that were now becoming routine. Jerry sensed that even if he stopped pushing, people would continue to work with the new system, rather than reverting to former ways. The work force as well as the work system had gained a new sense of balance.

While the internal changes in the plant were taking hold, external industry-wide events presented a new problem. The aviation industry was experiencing a major downturn in world-wide demand. Some slackening of sales had been anticipated, but recently the actual decline had been dramatic. Instead of feeling satisfaction over their current accomplishments, the Cunningham work force was beginning to feel fear and uncertainty. Would there be enough demand in the future for all the current aviation suppliers? Was Cunningham resourceful enough to survive a likely industry shakeout?

Jerry was affected by this turn of events; personally, he had his own fears about Cunningham and the industry as a whole. But he pushed his doubts aside and began to address a new set of business priorities. It was imperative that Cunningham secure its competitive position. Jerry's challenge would be to simultaneously maintain the current plant improvements while reducing costs.

With this cost containment issue coming to a head, it was difficult for Jerry to maintain his focus on the current Change

Cycle. But he was intent on guiding the original changes through to completion. The work force would have to focus on completing the current cycle of change while implementing the urgent new cost initiatives. It would put a strain on everyone, but it was absolutely necessary and unavoidable.

Jerry winced as he imagined the new complexities and stress that lay ahead. But he also was beginning to formulate a way to move from the current change effort to a new Change Cycle where cost reduction could be addressed. This would be a natural next step allowing Cunningham to respond to worrisome industry trends as well as to Advanced Aviation. Cunningham was in a much better position to reduce costs now that the new manufacturing process was virtually in place. Jerry was certain that there were ways to build a bridge between the current change effort and what was now needed.

Discussion

Whenever there are significant changes in an organization, the existing balance within the system is upset. Regardless of how beneficial the changes are, the sense of order and comfortable fit is altered. There comes a time when the new ways of doing things must be integrated with the remaining old ways.

This requires a rebalancing of major components of the system. It may mean that priorities must be shifted, or that new lines of communication must be established. It may require a different inventory system or new attitudes toward other departments. Whatever it takes, rebalancing cannot be completed until people try the new way of doing things. They must first experience what it's like to do things in the new way before they can fully grasp how these changes will affect the work system as a whole.

It is extremely difficult, if not impossible, to anticipate all the effects of a change on the functioning of a system before the change is actually made. Of course, many things can be anticipated and solid planning does pay off, but much remains to be learned as the change is actually made. As people experience what it is like to do their jobs in the new way, they will almost always run into problems fitting the new way together with the parts of their job that haven't changed. Whether it is difficulties with materials that aren't available when needed, or problems with co-workers who are fighting the new system, there always seem to be additional shifts in attitudes, systems, and action patterns needed before things can function in an integrated way. The major objectives of Stage Five, "Rebalancing", is to fit all the pieces together so that a renewed sense of balance is established.

Organizational Change Cycles do not occur in isolation. They are affected by unexpected events, shifts in priorities, and complexities of all sorts. It would be unrealistic to expect anything else. In Cunningham's case, there was interference during Stage Five due to industry-wide indications of a shrinking market. In order to successfully lead a change effort, there must be creative responses to the unexpected. The leader must also be able to maintain his own balance and cool-headed perspective in the face of personal doubts, complex challenges, and stress.

Stage Six: Reviewing the Transition and Leveraging the Learning

The stage was set for Jerry's next move. The original plant changes were largely in place and operating smoothly. It was time to step back from the implementation process and examine what had been accomplished, what had been learned, and what their next steps would be. Not only would people be looking back at the past, they would also be looking forward to what they must do in the future. This would be a natural place to address the urgency of securing a strong competitive position through lowering manufacturing costs.

Jerry decided to organize small task groups to evaluate specific aspects of the recent transition: the new assembly methods, the new product engineering approach, and the dedicated product teams. Each group was asked to review the entire transition from its assigned perspective. What had been tried? What had worked and what had failed? In either case, what did we learn? Given the chance, what would we do differently? What are our new capabilities and strengths, as we move forward?

Next the groups were to identify any unfinished business—remaining steps that were needed to complete the transition. Then, they would examine the current business situation to identify business priorities and challenges. The realties of a shrinking market, aggressive competition, and a likely industry shakeout would be part of this review. Finally, they would brainstorm new opportunities and possible next steps. What were they equipped to do now that they weren't equipped to do before the transition? What could they do now to build on the improvements just made? What priorities must they address to safeguard the future? Once they were finished, an overview committee would integrate all of this information.

Within three weeks, the overview group was able to draw conclusions and recommend a path forward. By now, the teams were feeling a sense of the magnitude of their past year's accomplishment. This was cause for celebration, even though they were also feeling the press of business realities.

While it was certain that cost reduction must be achieved, it was also apparent that new opportunities now existed as a result of all they had learned through the current Change Cycle. Cunningham now knew how to blend modern team assembly methods with precision hand adjustments. They could use this capability to build a wide variety of new products. Marketing had identified new product possibilities for commercial and pleasure boats. Long-term possibilities for research and design of high performance automotive products based on emerging technologies also looked promising. By adapting the same basic technology used for aviation instruments, the company was now primed to diversify into other markets. It was not yet clear how all of these needs and opportunities would be pursued, but people were now thinking positively about the future.

Discussion

Once people have developed new attitudes, skills, and methods, they can leverage this learning, using it as the foundation for the next Change Cycle. But this leveraging depends upon integrating what has been learned. People must be able to step back from their daily activities and pin down just what has changed in the way they think about their jobs, perform their work, and feel about the workplace. They must also look at what new skills and expertise they have gained, and how this new capability could be developed and used in the future.

Stage Six integration can include identifying a variety of new possibilities for future development. For example, it may be time to look again at an old idea whose time is ripe. Other possibilities may result from identifying new technological trends, or industry or market opportunities. New possibilities can also result directly from new skills, perspectives, product ideas, or expertise developed during the Change Cycle. Cunningham had developed new manufacturing expertise and instrument design concepts that could now be leveraged into new product lines.

In organizations, a formal consolidation process such as the one Jerry used is often needed. By examining not only what has been learned during the change effort, but also the implications of this learning for the future, the stage is set for movement forward. New capabilities allow the organization to stand on higher ground from which it can see farther; possibilities open up that weren't visible or thinkable before. It is hard to imagine a period of significant change where people don't learn something that can be leveraged into even greater accomplishments. Consolidating the learning of the past can be the beginning of a natural bridge between one cycle of change and the next. Cunningham was ready for Stage Seven.

Stage Seven: Completing the Cycle of Change and Transitioning to the Next Cycle

The overview committee was eager to present its results officially. Their findings had added up to much more than self-congratulatory accounts of what had transpired: they were building the bridge to the future. As the workers listened to the committee members lay out their findings, each one found meaning in the events of the last year, for each had undergone a personal transition. This event signaled the closure of a difficult period of change. For Jerry, it was a moment of culmination, after many years of dreaming about leading such an effort. For all, it was a bittersweet time; pride in their accomplishments was mixed with concern about the future.

At the same time, this event was opening the door on possible futures. Some in the audience smiled—wasn't this how they had gotten caught up in the changes of the past year and a half? There were immediate challenges: how quickly could cost initiatives be implemented? How rapidly could the current line of aviation instruments be modified to fit maritime markets? Could the engineers make the needed design changes? Can we gear up for producing a new line, building prototypes, and pre-marketing the product line in the next eighteen months? And down the road, the new arena of automotive devices would require quite a lengthy lead time for the necessary technology development. They were again in the position of having to juggle several important initiatives simultaneously. But going after these new markets, while reducing costs, was essential given the softening of the aviation market.

The committee was careful to save these revelations for last, in order not to distract from the important opportunity for people to reflect on what they had been through and what they had collectively accomplished. The strategy worked well. For all of the satisfaction people felt in hearing about past accomplishments, once that had been given its due, they became intrigued with what lay ahead: new possibilities, new opportunities, and the challenge of overcoming the industry slump. The confidence born of past success led this work force to feel more prepared to meet the challenges ahead. Although he had his concerns, Jerry couldn't help grinning as he imagined what the next couple of years would be like. He thrived on a challenge and planned on being there, every step of the way.

Discussion

The Seventh Stage, "Moving to the Next Cycle," refers to the moment when one Change Cycle ends and another begins. It is the moment when many of the things people have been thinking about and working on seem to gel into a recognizable whole. It is also the moment when people feel a clear impulse to leave the old cycle behind, and move into something new.

Reaching the last stage of a Change Cycle doesn't mean that you have accomplished everything you set out to do. There are almost always challenges left from the past to be dealt with in the future. But that doesn't take away from the tangible accomplishments and the feeling of satisfaction that exists at the transition point between one cycle and the next. Once this point is reached, everyone involved in the change effort recognizes that not only have they done something valuable, but they are ready to take the next step!

Chapter 3

Stages of the Change Cycle: Typical Issues

In each stage of the Change Cycle, small changes occur that progressively lead toward larger change. Although each change effort is unique, the types of issues that tend to arise within each stage remain fairly constant. Through examples and discussion, I'll introduce you to a few of these typical issues.

The examples below may help you to recognize and respond to specific kinds of problems, but let me offer two suggestions for getting more than that from these stories. First, pay less attention to specific solutions to problems than to the processes these managers use to get at those solutions. Second, notice how clearly defining a problem helps the manager recognize where a project is in the Change Cycle. Knowing where you are allows you to determine an appropriate response to the problems you confront there.

Every change process is different. Your response to the barriers you encounter needs to be yours. These examples are intended to help you "experience" how others have dealt with certain problems. You can learn from their successes and mistakes, as you work through each of these examples.

Automating Paper Flow:
An Example of Stages One and Two

Changes affecting how staff or employees perform work are difficult to implement when shifts in attitudes, values, and beliefs are also involved. Attitudes about how we do our work can be deeply ingrained. Yet these days, the worker for whom such change *isn't* occurring is a rarity. For better or worse, new technologies will continue to transform the way we do our jobs, and managers will continue to be called upon to implement those changes.

When introducing new and complex technologies, you can count on an uphill struggle. This is especially true when your change follows an earlier attempt that failed. In the following example, we'll observe the manager of a human services agency through the first two stages of such a remedial change process.

Stage One: Choosing the Target

The State Department of Human and Health Services was all but gridlocked by the inadequacies and the sheer mass of its paper records system. The solution was apparent to everyone: the agency needed a computerized records system. Unfortunately, two years earlier a former director had taken a disastrous step in this direction. The operating budget was depleted and the patience and motivation of agency staff were exhausted during that well-publicized debacle, and it cost the director his job.

Two years and two directors later, the agency had no choice but to move forward again with this effort. Unresolved pain, continually brought to the surface by poor results from the old manual system, made this new attempt a necessity. Rob Sullivan, assistant director of administration, was charged with making it work. Taking stock of his situation, Rob identified several problems:

◆   Like most managers, Rob didn't have the luxury of time for extended research. He also couldn't afford serious mistakes. He had to gather and assimilate what information he could in a reasonable time period, and to determine what the new computerized system should be like.

◆   Rob would likely have fewer resources than he thought were needed for implementing this change. The State had funded the prior effort. They could not be counted on for additional funding, in spite of the need and urgency. Rob suspected he would be asked for a plan that would work without an infusion of new resources.

♦ Management didn't know why the prior system had failed. The system itself appeared to be sound, and staff had been trained by the book. The whole process—development, testing, installation, user training, and follow-up—appeared to follow the conventional wisdom. Yet the system had been rejected by staff, who in the past two years had managed to revert almost entirely to their former paper systems. Rob was reluctant to start over without understanding what had gone wrong before.

For Rob, the last of these barriers was the first he needed to overcome—he had to understand what happened to subvert the use of the prior system. In search of answers, he reviewed documentation of the project, and talked at length with designers, the intended users, and their managers. He spent some time using the system with test data. He found pretty much what he'd expected:

♦ The system was technologically sound and reasonably user-friendly. Nothing in the design and function of the system explained its rejection. He could use the existing system as a base, with two exceptions. New agency procedures and programs would need to be incorporated, and recent technological advances could replace a few of the more cumbersome system features. The former design team agreed that a moderate upgrade should be developed before reestablishing the system agency-wide.

♦ The agency's needs had been inventoried and well understood during the design and testing phases of the project. As a result, those needs were accurately addressed by the system, and the agency's expectations were in line with the finished product. The problem didn't lie in a discontinuity between agency expectations and the delivered product.

♦ The original design team had staged the introduction of the new system appropriately, using widely accepted training and follow-up methods. They continued training even slow learners until everyone could operate the system independently.

As soon as the last user was established on-line, the project team and management, having accomplished what they set out to do, shifted their attention elsewhere. They continued to monitor and report on the system's effectiveness periodically, but the implementation process was declared complete.

As Rob reviewed his findings, something clicked. This wasn't an effort that had been problem-ridden from the outset, as some are. Instead, everything appeared to be going smoothly and the project seemed to have been successfully completed—until management and the project team turned their backs to attend to other pressing matters. But, Rob mused, they hadn't left the scene until the final steps of their work plan were carried out.

Rob thought he'd uncovered the fatal flaw. The project team's definition of its responsibility had seriously downgraded its chances for success. Both management and the team members had construed the design team's function mainly in terms of system design and development. They hadn't short changed training. But the work plan effectively ended when the last staff person was competent to use the system. Follow-up was scant, and it had been entirely directed at the technology.

Rob looked more closely at the records from this period. After the final scheduled training session, he noted, staff had gradually used the system less and less. Memos from that time were enlightening—managers were frustrated at staff for sidestepping an expensive system intended to help them be better organized and more productive; staff deftly dodged management's half-hearted attempts to force them to use the system, promising to try harder as soon as things slowed down a bit—which wasn't likely to happen by anybody's forecast. Within a year of its completion, as far as Rob could tell, the system was only marginally in use. Meanwhile, the problems it had been created to solve were multiplying.

When Rob presented his findings to his director, she was relieved at his analysis of the technology's integrity. With moderate upgrading, it should be usable, so the only remaining problem was how to get an updated system integrated into the agency's way of doing work.

With a clear idea of the problem, Rob was motivated to develop a solution. Rob had been trained in *Leading Change: Overcoming Chaos* techniques. He was familiar with the stages of change, so he was ready to translate these ideas into a plan for his project. One principle in particular seemed relevant to Rob, as he reviewed the failed process. A Change Cycle isn't considered complete—and change cannot be assumed permanent—until all changes are fully integrated into the workings of the organization, and new learning from the cycle is assimilated. The previous project had failed, Rob was convinced, because management and the team had quit before the cycle was complete.

Rob drafted a chart, outlining for each stage in the Change Cycle his desired outcomes, the principle barriers he expected to encounter, and appropriate actions he and others might take. His stage-by-stage chart wasn't a substitute for other planning tools, but an adjunct to these. The chart let him structure a definition of the challenges he would face and appropriate means for meeting them.

Chart 3. Rob's Plan for the Computerized Project Management System[1]

---

[1] *During any Change Cycle, it is more important to understand the general flow and sequence of actions than to be rigid about timing of specific actions. For example, a pilot project could occur in Stage Two as part of a planning effort, or in Stage Three as the first action of a rollout. Each change project will have its own unique step-by-step plan. Use these charts as guidelines, but allow yourself the room to flex as needed.*

STAGE ONE: CHOOSING THE TARGET

Desired Outcomes —————————————————————
- Agreement on the need to redesign and implement a new system
- Corporate sponsorship firmed up
- Preliminary vision of the new system up and running
- Understanding of the reasons the previous computer system failed to be accepted

Actions (Partial List) —————————————————
- Analyze previous effort to discover what went wrong and how to avoid similar problems
- Talk to people who designed and used the original computer system to determine the nature and extent of the changes needed
- Find a compelling way to express the shortcomings of the current system
- Overcome the resistance to try again by raising the level of discomfort and stimulating the desire to solve the problem
- Develop a descriptive statement of what the new system will be like once it is operating smoothly (vision statement)
- Determine what resources will be needed to design the new system and develop an implementation plan

Issues and Barriers to Overcome —————————————
- Memories of the previous failed effort to implement a similar system and resulting resistance among upper management as well as user groups
- People's reluctance to share what they really think went wrong, or their distorted memories of the project
- Resistance to sponsorship and committing the needed resources, based on mixed feelings (don't want to run the risk of another failure)

STAGE TWO: SETTING GOALS

Desired Outcomes

- Commitment of resources needed for design and implementation team (if this commitment wasn't gained in Stage One, it is needed now)
- More detailed vision of the new computerized system, based on new insights gained during the planning process
- Specific goals for the project; by accomplishing these goals, the vision is brought into reality
- Detailed implementation plan
- Plans for redesigned computerized project management system
- Pilot testing (if needed) well underway, if not completed
- Acceptance of the vision and implementation plan by the planning team, sponsors, and key managers of user groups
- Clarity on how much time, energy, and resources it will take to complete the change; may require additional commitments

Actions (Partial List)

- Form a design and planning team
- Create specific goals—how to accomplish the vision (done by the team)
- Do a thorough post-mortem on previous attempt; apply learnings to improve this effort and avoid repeating mistakes of the past
- Meet with key sponsors and users one-on-one as specific needs and requirements are identified (to help build their ownership and prepare them for approval of necessary resources); this is an ongoing task
- Redesign the computerized project management system

Issues or Barriers to Overcome

- Repeating the mistakes of the aborted system
- Perception that this effort will also fail
- Not having a strong enough planning team to do the job well (not enough skills and expertise)

STAGE THREE: INITIATING ACTION

Desired Outcomes

◆ Tangible results and benefits begin to appear (as results appear, they are identified, measured and shared)
◆ People feel more confident that this project can succeed
◆ Debugging of system completed (or nearly so)
◆ User training completed
◆ New system operating throughout department
◆ Ownership of the change effort shifting to the user groups

Actions (Partial List)

◆ Hold presentations and discussions (group and one-on-one as needed) with system users; share reasons for making the changes, expected results, and implementation plan.
◆ Give special attention to training user group managers: develop their sense of ownership and prepare them for leadership
◆ Relocate the project team temporarily to the user group area to assist in implementation
◆ Deliver training on how to use the system
◆ Startup the computer system throughout the work area.
◆ Deal with start-up problems, including possible design modifications
◆ Start to measure results and user response to the change; report results to users, sponsors and stakeholders

Issues or Barriers to Overcome

◆ Insufficient effort applied to transferring ownership out into organization
◆ Management expects too many results too soon
◆ Misperception that once the system is set in motion, the job is essentially complete; implementation problems not identified and resolved
◆ Implementation team diverted before changes become routine; resources not committed long enough to implement change
◆ Not enough skills or effort applied to overcome start-up problems

STAGE FOUR: MAKING CONNECTIONS

Desired Outcomes ─────────────────────────────
- All start-up bugs are out of the system
- Users are competent and comfortable managing their project information on the new computerized system
- People have begun to understand how the new way of managing projects fits into their job as a whole
- Benefits of the new way of doing things are apparent to users, sponsors, and other stakeholders
- Ownership of the change continuing to shift to the user groups, but still may not be complete

Actions (Partial List) ─────────────────────────
- Insure that users and managers understand how the new system affects all aspects of their work; evidenced by formal and informal discussions, experiments with new usage ideas, and memos between interfacing departments as they work things out
- Shift emphasis from getting the system running and getting everyone to use it, to making the system run smoothly and effectively; modify system and usage procedures based on user feedback
- Scrutinize results to determine if the benefits of the change are real

Issues or Barriers to Overcome ──────────────────
- Insufficient effort made to transfer ownership to user groups
- Users not given enough freedom or encouragement to discuss, think about, and experiment with the new system
- Tangible results and benefits are not measured and reported back to interested parties; without seeing the benefits of the change, momentum is lost, and the transfer of ownership may never be completed
- If the change doesn't yield enough tangible benefit by this stage, people will have serious doubts about its value
- Management supporters assume too early that change effort is complete, and shift attention to other projects

STAGE FIVE: REBALANCING TO ACCOMMODATE THE CHANGE

Desired Outcomes

- The change has become irreversible and self-sustaining
- Using the new system is now routine and shifts have occurred throughout the organization to accommodate it
- The new system is now functioning at a significantly higher level than the old manual methods
- Improved results are now apparent and hard to refute

Actions (Partial List)

- Help managers of the user groups develop and implement their own action plan to overcome barriers at this stage (done by the project team)
- The project team and line managers monitor the situation to make sure rebalancing is occurring throughout the organization; intervene where necessary
- Identify whether the new computer system affects the way staff deals with clients and other departments
- Make sure results are being identified and compared objectively to results prior to the change; report to all

Issues and Barriers to Overcome

- The project team may want to pull out or may get reassigned before the change has become self-sustaining, or before their role has been adequately supplanted by the user groups (watch for this in Stages Three and Four, as well)
- Celebrating the change before sufficient proof of the benefits has occurred.
- Not enough attention paid to the impact of the change outside the primary user groups: ripple effects throughout the organization; changes needed elsewhere in the organization to complete the rebalancing effort

STAGE SIX: CONSOLIDATING THE LEARNING

Desired Outcomes

◆ Clear understanding of what was accomplished versus what we set out to do: what worked, what didn't, and reasons why

◆ Possibilities for the future are identified; some of these may be direct by-products of what was accomplished and learned making this change

◆ All interested parties know what we've accomplished and what opportunities now exist for the future

◆ A feeling of accomplishment for all who were involved; people are looking forward to what comes next

Actions (Partial List)

◆ Set up a consolidation committee to pull together information on what has been accomplished, what did and did not work, and what's next

◆ Collect the best ideas for the future from a large sample of people who took part in the change effort

◆ Organize a formal process to disseminate what has been learned, and to celebrate accomplishments; make sure we also look forward to what comes next—the new opportunities and challenges

Issues and Barriers to Overcome

◆ People don't see the value of consolidation and short-cut this step

◆ Not enough people participate, resulting in less leveraging of what we've gained

◆ Failure to pin down and publicize good results leaves people without understanding what they have accomplished and leaves the door open for unwarranted devaluing of the change and resistance to future efforts

◆ People focus only on the completed project without identifying future possibilities; momentum is lost

STAGE SEVEN: MOVING TO THE NEXT CYCLE

Desired Outcomes
- We are ready to tackle new challenges
- We are excited about the new possibilities
- We have a sense of completion combined with forward momentum

Actions (Partial List)
- Find a compelling way to talk about what lies ahead, as well as what's just been done
- Begin defining a concrete process to move into the next cycle

Issues or Barriers to Overcome
- Getting stuck on the cusp of a new cycle, because we lack forward momentum; not enough excitement about future possibilities
- Treating this as an end point, instead of a transition
- Thinking that all we can do now is make refinements to what we have already done—selling ourselves short

As Rob reviewed his chart, the notion of participation and transferring ownership surfaced. He followed this line of thought. Certain key individuals or groups would need to feel ownership at each point during the cycle. He noted when project responsibilities and roles would need to shift for this to happen. Rob also recognized that interactions with various parts of the agency ought to be changing in predictable ways from stage to stage. The change process couldn't be completed unless the project team and management succeeded in transferring a share of the project commitment and ownership to an increasing number of participants throughout the Change Cycle.

Rob projected that during the latter stages of the project, some staff would be integrating the system into their day-to-day functioning, while others would be ready to reflect on what had been accomplished. This second group could be engaged in considering any interesting implications of the new system for the future of the agency. And finally, because he believed that feedback loops had been inadequate in the earlier effort, Rob identified who needed feedback, when it would be most important, and how it would be given.

Rob had a fairly clear picture by now of how the agency could function with the new system in place, and he had ideas about how to stabilize use of the new technology. He felt ready to share his vision with others. First, he took a moment to evaluate the present status of his project:

◆   The agency director had committed to him that she would go forward with the project, although she would only marginally fund the effort.

◆   The agency director and the other assistant directors, however, were solidly behind Rob's effort, in spite of the previous bad experience, and they felt his early hypothesis about the reasons for the prior failure were plausible. Desperation may have had something to do with this, but that would do for motivation.

◆   Those who were still with the agency from the original project team, including the MIS division head, were eager to redeem themselves. The resurrection of this project raised some anxiety but, on the whole, it was well received in this department.

◆ Rob understood the likely causes for the failure of the first system.

◆ Even staff, while skeptical, were ready for resolution of the tensions created by the failed effort and the mounting paper chaos. There wasn't exactly a ground swell of support at this early stage—no one knew enough to have confidence in the new effort—but neither was there great resistance.

The issues of Stage One were about as well resolved as they could be. Rob had entered the scene as part of the agency's initial commitment. His full-time assignment to the project, and the temporary assignment of his lead manager as assistant director for all other administrative functions, represented the initial investment. In terms of the Change Cycle model, the director's acceptance of his findings and her initial commitment to his vision statement and recommendation to move ahead represented the fruition of Stage One, "Choosing the Target", and the transition to Stage Two, "Setting Goals".

Stage Two: Setting Goals

During Stage Two, the project becomes more clearly defined. With that definition comes a reality check on all the resources necessary to complete the project. Commitment of the resources necessary to bring about change is a critical test of the will of the group to make the change happen... as Rob is about to discover.

Rob was able to build on the earlier team's work from his general sense of the past effort and present-day needs. But solid as that was, he wanted to clear his mind of preconceptions, to develop a fresh viewpoint and approach based on contemporary data. He was ready to get a strong team together, but decided it wasn't essential that the team be organized before his data was gathered and he had more fully formulated his own vision. With the agency's limited resources in mind, Rob elected to continue alone for now. With this decision, he accepted an obligation: to accurately and completely convey what he learned to the team once it was formed, so this work wouldn't have to be repeated by them. Rob realized he would need to share with his future team all the reasons leading to a second try for a new computer system. Also the team members would need a chance to work through doubts, objections, and residue from the past that could interfere in this new attempt. With this in mind, Rob spent a little more time with a few end users—case workers, their support staff, and their immediate supervisors. He observed these staff in action, and tried to do the same system-related tasks they would perform. From all of this, he formulated a more complete and accurate vision of the new system in action. Rob refined his earlier conclusions:

- ◆ The system as designed was fundamentally sound. Changes in agency procedures and new technological opportunities made it attractive, if not imperative, that the agency invest in a good upgrade effort.

- ◆ The earlier training and implementation effort had been good as far as it went, but it had ended prematurely. Rob wanted the agency's commitment not only to training for staff, but to a well-planned follow-up period. This renewed change process would have to be well designed and fully staffed, until the project was completely through the Change Cycle.

Rob spent a couple of days fine-tuning his vision of the fully integrated and functioning new system. He wasn't concerned with details—that was to be his planning team's role—but with his overall sense of how the agency would function, how the system would fit into the way tasks were accomplished, and the effect it would have on end users' working patterns. Once he was clear, he would be able to communicate his preliminary vision to his planning team. He wanted his team to be involved in shaping the final vision, so that they would grow in ownership of the project. Rob expected that his team members would have useful additions, and their shared vision would be better than his first attempt. Their task would then be to develop a solid set of goals and an implementation plan, and then to help him communicate the goals and plan throughout the agency. He looked forward to the day that nearly everyone in the agency would share the same vision, working together toward the same desired outcome.

Rob now felt that his director would have to up the ante a bit on her commitment. Clear about what he hoped to accomplish and convinced that he knew how to do it, Rob was eager to organize his planning and design team. He wanted a group with cross-functional skills to define goals for the project, anticipate problems, and develop solutions. Using this approach early in the redesign process would allow the group to accomplish quality conceptual work, reducing the number of problems they would encounter when they started field testing the new system.

Rob put together his ideal team on paper, then went to his director to get the assignments approved. Unfortunately, what Rob wanted and what he got were two entirely different things. Rob was asking for one good person from each of four key divisions, all but one of whom now were in supervisory positions. The fifth member was an MIS supervisor known for his personal skills as well as his competence in systems design.

To Rob's surprise, the director could not—or would not—commit any of these people to the project. Rob could tap their expertise as needed, if he could convince them to participate as time allowed. But the director felt each was too valuable for even part-time assignment to the project. As it turned out, the director had in mind a change process that Rob would carry out for the most part by himself. When she agreed that Rob would have the staff time he needed, she had expected his need to be for MIS time for minor upgrading of the system and supplemental training. She was already uncomfortable with reports of how much staff time was being taken up by Rob's research.

Essentially, as they discussed his request, Rob realized that the director's model for this change process was fairly simplistic: if nothing fatal had been found wrong with the system so far, then bring it up to speed quickly, retrain as needed, and enforce its use. She wasn't inclined to devote much more time to planning, much less to an extended implementation effort. The job could be done, she insisted, by a couple of their best systems designers with the support and cooperation of the rest of the agency. Surely Rob could obtain all the information and assistance he needed by connecting up with the appropriate division heads. This was, after all, a clearly stated priority item in the agency—one of the top ten. Rob should have no problem getting the information and support he needed for this project from them.

Rob was stunned. Not only was his base of support a lot thinner than he'd thought, he felt misled. This same director had promised him assistance and resources; to Rob, that translated into people, equipment, time, and some level of funding. Now she seemed to be putting the whole burden on his shoulders. How was he supposed to control this project and move it along with this scant level of support? When it really counted, the agency's commitment had virtually evaporated.

At least these were some of Rob's initial thoughts, certainly colored by his emotions of the moment. But upon reflection, using the change process model as a reality check, Rob was able to see this situation from another perspective. Stage Two in the change process is a time for testing commitment. Rob had defined the effort, the resource requirements became clearer, and the agency's commitment needed to be turned up a few notches to match the project's needs. This was a natural time in the cycle for the agency's level of commitment to be tested. The problem Rob faced was part of the process, not the result of anyone misleading him—or themselves.

Rob's mood softened as he realized that most projects face similar tests. The rejection of his staffing proposal was not a rejection of his efforts to date. Neither was it a sign of under-handed methods or vacillation on the part of his director. The sting of personal rejection and doubts about the motives of upper management dissipated, Rob regained his composure and objectivity. He merely faced a barrier typical of Stage Two in any change effort. He needed to evaluate his own commitment to proceeding, then plot his strategy and tactics to meet the challenge.

In this case, Rob's assignment didn't change. He was still expect-ed to make the project happen, and he believed in it. His personal commitment remained firm. He decided to wait a little before pressing his demand for full-time resources. He could familiarize himself more with the problems to be addressed by the new system, and identify staff who might really want to work with him on the project, regardless of whether or not they were formally assigned. Rob figured that there was enough pain in the organization over these operational problems that several people would, of their own free will, want to do something about the situation.

If he could enlist support early on, he could get the project moving, building momentum. He might then be able leverage this support to revisit the question of resources with upper management. Even if they turned him down again, he'd be in a position to move ahead with the support generated on his own. Rob liked this idea, and thought he had little to lose, so long as he stayed reasonably within his current means and if he maintained a fairly low profile with his bids for more direct support.

He also reasoned that if he couldn't generate any substantive support among the user group, he'd have cause to bring the issue of commitment to a head. In this way, the required project would either receive the expanded commitment it needed or be dropped altogether. The question immediately at hand was whether he could get any others involved. Could the obvious potential of an excellent computer support system place high enough on anyone's wish list for them to commit their time?

Rob in his own way was pushing for resolution of this Stage Two issue. If he didn't succeed, he'd know that he had gone as far as he could. He'd done his best to understand and address the issues that would face virtually anyone in his position. While the seven-stage Change Cycle hadn't given Rob ready-made solutions, it had given him the perspective to define, understand, and act on the problem. Rob had already developed a vision of a new system that would solve his agency's problems. He had also identified major barriers to implementation and ways to overcome them.

Note that we're leaving Rob midway into Stage Two. If the project does survive, Rob will complete Stage Two when the agency commits to provide adequate resources for the project, when his team sets goals and develops the implementation plan, and when the system designers complete the modifications.

In any change process, we face barriers that must be overcome if we're to succeed. The seven-stage Change Cycle model helps us to understand the driving and restraining forces operating at each stage of the cycle. The utility of this tool is illustrated as we continue to work through a variety of change management issues in the following examples.

Quality Control in Market Research:
An Example of Stage Three

Let's look at Stage Three of a Change Cycle in a large market research company that is initiating a quality control program. Joyce Schuster, vice-president of consumer research at Pacific Market Research, faces a crisis: one of her biggest clients has questioned the validity of a recent Pacific consumer survey.

The client is a manufacturer of trendy women's clothing. He argued that Pacific's latest data on teen preferences and buying behavior is inconsistent with other data, and that Pacific's data could have led to some very expensive mistakes had not one of the client's own staff caught the discrepancies. Joyce was professionally embarrassed, a position she never wanted to be in again. After a grueling conference with her client, she corralled her research staff and asked them to pull together all documentation on the project in question.

Among other things, she reviewed the survey methodology. Almost immediately, her practiced eye caught the problem. The wording of several questions on the consumer survey was ambiguous, a flaw that would almost certainly account for seriously skewed results. Tracking the history of this questionnaire, she found no evidence of a pretest. This early opportunity to discover and correct problems had been missed, and then a second omission had also occurred. While coding the survey, her research assistants should have been cued by inconsistencies in answers—inconsistencies that clearly indicated possible problems. Even that late in the game, she could have scratched the survey results instead of sending them to the client.

Joyce's job was to bring in new business. She wasn't ordinarily involved in projects until the results were presented to the client.

She counted heavily on her research team, and the problems in the survey process plus the failure of her staff to forestall the distribution of inaccurate data was a clear signal that her policy of expecting quality control from research supervisors had to be revisited.

When Joyce brought her problem to Pacific's president, she found she wasn't alone with this issue. Hers was the last in a series of similar incidents, the others on a smaller scale, that seemed to indicate a growing need for change. Pacific's product was credible information. If word got out that Pacific was selling questionable information, business would disappear virtually overnight. The president, the vice-president of industrial research, and Joyce collaborated on developing tight new policy and procedures for quality control, and planned to implement these as rapidly as possible.

Together, the three of them completed Stage One, "Choosing a Target", and Stage Two, "Setting Goals". The procedures the team had developed were ready to go. Joyce was eager to take the plan back to her supervisors and to move into Stage Three. However, Joyce's concern and competence moved the president to ask her to assume more responsibility—to lead the entire company in this change effort. Joyce's job was to implement the quality control measures not just in her own unit, but with all project directors, research assistants, and data entry personnel.

Stage Three: Initiating Action

Joyce was asked to train her colleagues in the new procedures. As a student of *Leading Change: Overcoming Chaos,* she realized that successful training entailed more than a series of informational meetings and training sessions. While Joyce felt commitment to the new quality control measures, she would need to transfer the sense of ownership to all participants.

She began her action plan with a communication strategy. Everyone knew about the faulty research. The staff involved in that project and those who'd had similar experiences were feeling defensive; the rumor mill had been churning while the three leaders were planning for change. Joyce's first priority was reassurance: all employees needed to know that upper management assumed responsibility for procedures that had permitted the problems to occur, and now upper management was assuming responsibility for reorganizing to prevent future occurrences. No other individuals were to bear blame.

Next, she spent a half day with mid-level managers and supervisors. Here, she continued to spread the message of upper-management accountability, and started her training. She gave a factual run-down of the problems with her client and of the other incidents that pointed to the need for change. Then she presented the solution that upper management had developed. Each department was to organize a multi-disciplinary team to oversee all phases of research, bringing objectivity and a wider skill base to each project. Procedurally, however they chose to do it, every new research instrument was to be pretested—no exceptions. While the change was underway, senior staff would review all research plans, instruments, and reports before anything left the company.

This meeting put rumors to rest and allowed the supervisory staff to get their questions answered. Joyce stressed the positive: this was a chance to refine their product, to leverage the talents of each employee through teamwork. Next, Joyce followed up with one-on-one discussions, to bring each supervisor to the point of comfort with and belief in the new plan. In Change Cycle terms, she guided the supervisors through their personal Stages One and Two, so they could all move forward through Stage Three together.

All did not go smoothly; two of the seven supervisors presented problems. An industrial project supervisor was especially defensive. He disagreed with the conclusions of the small planning committee, maintaining that since his group had never produced faulty research, they shouldn't have to adopt the new procedures. Joyce met with him several times, to hear his concerns and to share details of the committee's process and decision making. At the end of the time she permitted for this process—not to mention at the end of her patience—Joyce still found herself confronted with an openly hostile supervisor who refused to institute the new system in his work group. When he found that upper management was intent on enforcing the new protocols, he let it be known that he was looking for a job elsewhere. Although Joyce was frustrated by her failure to reach him, she also felt relieved. He was making a clean separation by leaving, rather than remaining to subvert the change from within.

Her work with the second resistant supervisor was more fruitful. Once he was assured that his data entry group wasn't being singled out for change, he conceded that the new procedures would assure overall higher quality, improving the performance of his work group. Having realized the value of the change, he was willing to implement it.

With the supervisors involved in the change process, Joyce had succeeded in transferring a share of the ownership in the project to them. They picked up the effort, and scheduled unit meetings for Joyce to speak with their work groups. The meetings were similar in intent and format to the supervisory meeting; Joyce and the supervisors shared information and worked to gain staff understanding and commitment to the new plan.

Predictably, some staff saw value in the changes and committed to the new methods; other resisted, for a variety of reasons. But with practice in using the new methods and with feedback, supplemented by one-on-one meetings as needed, people generally accepted the change. Joyce's planning paid off. She held meetings for employee participation in testing and refining the new procedures, further spreading the sense of ownership. What could have been an onerous change for many turned out to be an exercise of their individual and team creativity.

Joyce responded well to one of the major issues arising during Stage Three, "Initiating Action". When broadening the project to include participants in the middle stages of any change process, the participants need time to catch up with the change leaders. This work entails more than merely informing participants that changes will be made and teaching them how to make them. Share the vision: What will the changes look like when they're completed? What are the benefits? Give people a chance to question and critique, understand, accept, and support the target and the intermediate goals. Every participant needs personally to work through Stages One and Two before being expected to implement change effectively.

In this example, the Stage Three work was accomplished when Joyce's organization proved its collective commitment and capability to institute a change. At the completion of Stage Three in any Change Cycle, change leadership will have tangible evidence of the participants' ability and willingness to move forward. Stage Four then follows, providing time for that ability and willingness to mature.

Assembly Lines to Assembly Teams: An Example of Stage Four

During Stage Four, change leadership needs to monitor, reinforce, and nurture forward movement, encouraging everyone's ongoing involvement in fine-tuning the new system. No matter how extensive your team-building and training effort has been or how effective the initial implementation has been, making incorrect assumptions that everyone has bought into the change and has figured out how the change fits into their jobs can be detrimental to your change effort. Let's follow the change process through Stage Four, "Making Connections", at a plant that manufactures heavy-duty farm vehicles.

Over a year ago, responding to quality problems, management at Iowa Tractor and Farm Equipment undertook a project to adapt a successful method from a leading automobile manufacturer for constructing major vehicle components. They had abandoned the assembly line in favor of a team approach to assembly. The automotive manufacturer had already borne most of the risk associated with the new approach, which now was proven cost-effective and conducive to high-quality finished products.

The change effort leadership moved through Stages One and Two, emerging with a clear definition of the desired outcome and a step-by-step implementation plan for their plant; the organization passed the commitment test, by dedicating appropriate resources to the project. In Stage Three, the change leaders began involving supervisors, foremen, and technicians. A pilot assembly team tested and refined the new procedures in preparation for plant-wide implementation. Meanwhile, all factory employees who would ultimately work on similar teams were being prepared: listening to presentations about the concept, viewing and discussing a video showing the system in operation in similar plants, and getting regular progress reports and personal feedback from the pilot team. Numerous small-group and one-on-one discussions were held to help people come to grips with the impending changes.

The final assembly teams were formed and walked through the new process. Each team took one chassis and installed all the remaining parts—engine, body, drive train, and so forth. In effect, the team adopted a particular vehicle and took responsibility for its quality and integrity. Management looked on as this process built each team's assembly skills, teamwork, and a sense of pride and ownership. The teams began using their combined skills to attack any problems that arose. The change process was making the transition from Stage Three, "Initiating Action", to Stage Four, "Making Connections", with hardly a ripple.

Stage Four: Making Connections

On the surface, everything seemed to be moving forward smoothly. However, a significant problem typical of this stage of change was emerging. Management thus far had invested an intense effort and considerable resources in this change project. They'd taken pains to do everything the right way from the outset, convinced that an intensive up-front effort would propel them through to the desired outcome with the fewest detours possible. In some respects, they were right. The investment was likely to pay off.

But management had already worked harder at implementing this change than any other in their lives. They'd stuck to the operating principle of "no surprises".[2] Although they were savvy enough to talk about success in terms of their "cautious optimism,"

---

[2] See pages 107–108 for a discussion of "no surprises" as a communications principle.

they were more than ready for the payoff now. This impatience primed them to selectively view the evidence before them, and they mistook surface calm for proof of success. Just when they needed to attend to nuances day-by-day, to subtle indicators of underlying problems, management was anticipating an end to this change process.

Two teams were starting the new system on-line. They'd trained together for this, and at first everything seemed to go well. Preliminary results were encouraging. High-quality vehicles were already being produced at a reasonable rate. Some of the usual start-up problems were being resolved. The unit managers seemed confident that results would keep improving as people mastered the new assembly procedures. But a few weeks into the process, personal conflicts started to flare up in one of the teams. Assuming that this signaled one of the anticipated teething problems of any new system, the human resources rep assigned to the team reacted accordingly, with individual counseling, role clarification, and team-building exercises. Several weeks later, in spite of these efforts, the tension within the group hadn't subsided. In fact, several members of the team simply wanted out. They wanted to return to their old jobs. And if that wasn't possible, they asserted, they would look elsewhere for employment.

This wasn't a terminal problem. But unattended, it could have undermined the whole project. What went wrong? Could this problem have been anticipated and avoided? Such rejection isn't an uncommon problem during the roll-out process. By the time any change process reaches this point, everyone has thought seriously about the change. They know without a doubt that the change is coming, and that they'll be expected to deal with it.

Once people are using new methods, the potential for rejection exists—especially if the transfer of ownership has been insufficient prior to the roll out. If Stage Three makes a change in some form an inescapable part of life—"it's here now"—then Stage Four will put the change to the acid test—"how well can it work in practice?" This is the moment of truth, and all eyes are on the arena where the change is being implemented.

Once past the start-up period, with major flaws in the new system corrected, attention can shift to a more advanced question: not "will it work?" but "how well can it work?" This is when the problem arose for Iowa Tractor. In this case, the flare-up among team members could be traced to discontent with the new assembly methods. At Iowa Tractor, the change was pushed forward before all the team members had a strong sense of ownership in the change.

Lack of ownership may be difficult to detect. Management's desire to call the project a success can lead to unintentionally premature assessments of the readiness of the work force and can create serious problems. Individual work responsibilities may not be changed enough to make it easy to catch deviations from new procedures. The preparation that had taken place at this plant was excellent, but had failed to achieve one vital objective: that each person who would participate in the change truly accepted it.

Workers need more than to understand why change is being made. They need more than an understanding of the potential benefits and new skills. A critical point occurs (or doesn't occur) when each person's point of view shifts regarding any new idea or method. In effect, each person must reach that point of saying "yes" to the change in order to fully support it. The connections between the effects of the change and the rest of their work lives must be made successfully.

When this doesn't happen, people can resist a new system in many ways, covert and overt. When a new way of doing things involves close interaction with others, as with a team approach to assembly, it's hard to keep one's opinions and feelings concealed. In the example above, the plant was lucky to have the problem emerge visibly, rather than have it insidiously subvert the change attempt, as often happens.

There is no magic solution to the question of what kind of and how much interaction is enough. This is simply a cautionary tale; the moral is to continue to pay attention through this stage of change. Your people must make an internal shift in their points of view; they must feel like co-owners of the new system. When they in effect say "yes" to the proposed changes, then implementation has a far greater chance for success.

In order to assure that the change is truly being supported, managers must continually monitor many factors. One important factor that is often overlooked is the informal communications network. What do workers say to each other while off-line or when their supervisors are not around? What rumors are creeping into the grapevine regarding how well the change is working? Keeping in touch with this informal communications network is a good way to identify potential problems before they erupt into real ones.

There are also particular people that may require special attention throughout the entire Change Cycle, but especially during the implementation stages. One such group includes individuals who put up the strongest resistance to any change effort, no matter how much it is needed or how well it is orchestrated. They are likely to have difficulty, no matter how well the change process is evolving overall. They may also be the individuals who spread unwarranted doubt about the change. Because resistance to change is so much a part of their nature, the objections they raise can be strongly felt and powerfully expressed, regardless of the validity of their points. Special attention is called for: private discussions where they can air their issues and get answers without disrupting others, and more individual processing of the implementation process as it affects their jobs in particular. It may also help to stage the change effort so that change-resistant individuals are the last ones to make the changes, thereby benefiting from the experience of others and smoothing their own process.

Another group of people who should receive special attention are thought leaders. These are the individuals who are particularly influential in shaping the opinions of others. They can affect others both positively and negatively. If these people become supporters of the change, they can persuade others. If they are against the change, or feel slighted by the way the change was managed, they can become formidable blockers. One way to gain their support is to involve them as early as possible in the Change Cycle. For example, they may be able to provide valuable practical knowledge and insights into how work is done and how it can be improved while plans are being developed.

Zero Monologues:
An Example of Stage Five

I'd like to share two examples for Stage Five. Both show the need for integration of a change, whether it is one person solving a personal problem at work or a group learning to use a new system. When change is a one-person effort, problems such as we saw in the example above are less likely to crop up during the Change Cycle. After all, only one person has to be convinced of the value of the change, allocate resources, and muster his own capability. Communication problems are certainly minimized.

But personal change has its own pitfalls, as we all know from personal experience. In our next example, we'll watch what typically goes wrong during Stage Five, "Rebalancing to Accommodate the Change", as someone tries to change a personal behavior pattern that was affecting his performance at work.

Frank had gradually become aware of a habit that had been getting worse over recent months: his tendency toward extended monologues, especially at work. He realized, through the intervention of a friend, that when he launched into one of his well-intentioned but lengthy explanations, his audience quickly turned off. Regardless of how good his ideas were or how well stated his case, his relentless lecturing soon produced glazed stares from most people. Frank understood that his effectiveness on his job was increasingly hampered by this behavior pattern, and so he decided to change it.

Watching himself for a time to see when and how this pattern emerged, Frank discovered that his monologues were triggered most often when he was trying to prove himself in a room filled with technically competent people. He would feel a strong impulse to share his knowledge—and he did. In the past, his ability to give clear and comprehensive explanations had been an asset. Now that it was out of control, this asset was becoming a liability. Frank didn't care what was at the root of this problem from a psychological perspective; he just wanted to solve it as quickly as he could.

Frank disliked the idea that he was turning people off by the way he shared his ideas, and he certainly didn't care for the fact that this pattern was interfering with his effectiveness at work. He set a straightforward objective for himself: zero monologues.

Frank's wife told him that she'd read about visualization techniques that athletes used to improve their performance. Although it sounded a little farfetched to Frank, he tried what his wife called thought experiments: he imagined himself in a few of the stickier situations at work that seemed to trigger his unwanted behavior. In his head, he ran a few "movies" of himself behaving differently. Just before the monologue was about to start, he held back to think of an appropriate response to the triggering event.

What does this person need most right now? How can I express it most effectively for him? As his movie went on, Frank saw himself delivering clear, succinct responses that really helped other people. He saw himself addressing their needs, not his own. He also envisioned their flashes of insight and their appreciation for his efforts.

Frank's action plan was simple and direct: apply the "zero monologue" procedure at work. He would monitor his own behavior and record all deviations from the course he'd set to reach his goal. He would try his best to perform on his job as he had imagined himself doing in his movies. For the next several weeks, Frank persisted, sometimes succeeding, sometimes not, but making steady progress. He found when he talked less, he listened better and related more to others. His behavior gradually came closer to his vision.

Frank ran fairly rapidly through the first four stages in his Change Cycle. But then he made a critical miscalculation. He had proved to his satisfaction that he could change his behavior. As he became less of a problem to others, the negative feedback that had spurred his change diminished. With diminishing negative feedback, Frank became less vigilant, assuming he could count on the new behavior to be his dominant mode. Within weeks, he slipped back into delivering lectures in response to co-workers' questions, and they began avoiding him again.

Stage Five is a period of time during which attention must be given to allowing the change to become an integrated, balanced part of a system. Frank needed to persist for another few weeks for the new pattern to become harmonized with the other patterns of his life. Without continuing attention while this balancing takes place, slippage can happen quickly. Once a change process reaches Stage Five, all that is essential to complete the cycle is continued drive and vigilance.

Frank's experience illustrates a common shortcoming in many attempts at making change, not just personal change. Breakdowns in the change process are manageable, especially during the later stages. The key is to remain aware that these later stages exist, that the cycle isn't complete once the desired change is first mani-fested. Because of the importance of this point, let's look at a similar example of Stage Five "Rebalancing", in a business setting.

A New Planning Process for a Marketing Team: Another Example of Stage Five

The marketing staff at a computer software company had been trained in a new systematic planning process that was far more demanding than previous methods. During the training, every-one was impressed with the new process. This method included more rigorously defining goals, objectives, and rationales, and creating detailed work plans. The marketing staff felt that this planning tool would help them implement a complex strategy for a new product introduction.

The training session included plenty of practice. People completed exercises designed to help them apply the system to some of their projects at work. By practicing the new techniques, the marketing staff realized the value of the process and they experienced using the tools. Trainers critiqued each person's practice exercises and worked with participants to create sample plans. At the end of the training, these managers felt ready to use the new procedures.

The marketing staff came back to work, excited about using the system. For one week, trainers were available to help them actually use these new techniques. At the first planning meeting for introducing and marketing their recently upgraded software product, the new procedures were used to define overall plans for the group. Each manager was then to use the same procedures to detail their own work unit plans. During this first week, all of the managers made use of the on-site trainers to help them develop these plans. In this way, planning for Phase One of the new product introduction was completed. Virtually all of the employees in the marketing group felt this new planning process to be a real advantage, and one that had clarified the complex job they were undertaking.

However, within a few weeks this initial enthusiasm died down. In reality, once the on-site trainers were gone, the press of the day-to-day demands overwhelmed the good intentions of many of these people. Because the new planning process was challenging and took time, most fell back on their familiar old methods within a month or two. Most of the plans for Phase Two were completed without the help of the new system.

In terms of the Change Cycle, this group had gone through Stage Four, "Making Connections", and had just arrived at Stage Five, "Rebalancing". However, these managers failed to make the new procedures a normal part of the way they worked. Even though they had been able to make significant shifts in their behavior patterns, these new patterns hadn't been established long enough to stabilize or fully integrate with the other patterns in the workplace.

Put simply, it wasn't yet part of the normal way of doing things. What might have helped is some extra time and attention to let the new behaviors settle in. During this period, a few more projects needed to be carefully guided through the new procedures before assuming that the changes had taken hold. This situation exemplifies many incomplete Change Cycles. Again, a little more awareness of the fragility of the change at the beginning of the fifth stage can make all the difference.

Improving Client Service: An Example of Stage Six

Stage Six has its own rewards and purpose. In this stage, you take time to step back, taking in all that has been accomplished, refocusing on any outstanding problems, and thinking about possibilities for the future.

At this point, you're in a position to measure or examine what has, in fact, changed. By the end of Stage Five, the change has been balanced and harmonized with other existing patterns. Rebalancing precedes reflection. Now you can determine how close you are to completion. Has the original vision been realized? If not, what remains to be accomplished? What are the implications for the future, given the change that has already occurred, plus any additional shifts as this change settles in? What else has been or will be affected by this change? Auditing the change— reflecting on your progress after rebalancing—anchors everyone's understanding of what has really happened, and what hasn't happened. Next steps, if any, become clear; you feel near to completion.

What happens if Stage Six is omitted? At this late stage, the stabilized change will probably hold. As long as the fifth stage has been adequately completed, and nothing major happens to topple the balance, a relatively permanent change can remain in place. Let's look at another example.

Stage Six: "Consolidating the Learning."

When Mark McClellan was appointed director of a Southwest regional budget office for federal health and human services programs, he inherited an organization with a poor reputation. Under his predecessors, the budget office was known for its unresponsiveness and uncaring attitude toward its client agencies. In contrast, Mark was committed to fiscal responsibility, and he believed that excellence in client service was the key to meeting that commitment. Within a month of his arrival, he'd chosen and communicated the target for his change.

Mark's budget office was aiming for consistent, cost-effective budgetary assistance to its client agencies. He formed a team of representatives from each fiscal unit. The team's assignment:

assess the strengths and weaknesses of the agency, then set specific goals that would lead to the target. Overall, the team determined that the agency had a fine performance record from an accounting perspective. Over the past twenty years, they had passed every audit with flying colors.

The agency's weakness, as predicted, was in client service. Mark and his team refined their understanding of the problems, and then set goals that ended up sounding a lot like performance standards:

◆   Every client contacting the office, regardless of the triviality or complexity of the query, was to be regarded as a client whose agency wanted to be fiscally responsible—behavior the budget office would acknowledge, encourage, and reward.

◆   Every client was entitled to reach the person who could best answer the question, make a decision, or provide the technical assistance with as little delay as possible, regardless of who that person might be.

◆   If a problem couldn't be solved with one contact, the client was entitled to know when the staff would get back with the necessary help, and then have that expectation met.

The team identified two barriers to hitting the target that Mark had set. The technological barrier was the office's obsolete telephone system. That could be replaced, and Mark put a smaller task force to work on selecting and recommending the appropriate system.

The second barrier was human—the culture that had grown around an hierarchical, enforcement model of government. Mark attacked that barrier personally, one-on-one and in groups, consistently making his expectations clear; hearing and responding to people's concerns and overcoming their objections; providing communication and client service training where needed; modeling the attitudes he wanted his staff to internalize. By the time the new phone system was chosen and installed and staff were comfortably using its new features, the technology and the culture were fairly well down the path to change together. A few months later, from an internal perspective, the changes had become unremarkable, part of the routine.

Client agencies did notice a few differences—they weren't being transferred and inadvertently disconnected nearly as often, for starters—and some nice feedback on specific instances of quick, effective problem solving was reaching Mark. But the positive feedback was less than expected. More perplexing, the rate of serious complaints remained at about the same level that it had been eighteen months ago, when Mark first arrived.

This news was discouraging, to say the least. Staff's tendency to blame the clients, characterizing them as fiscally irresponsible bleeding hearts, began to re-emerge. But Mark wasn't ready to give up so easily. He called a meeting of his original group to review the history of the change process, consolidating what had been learned, groping for an understanding of what had been missed. During this process, Mark noticed a wide discrepancy between the number of calls per month handled by first- and second-level staff compared with the number that managers typically handled. Some gap was appropriate, but this was more like a gulf. The managers seemed to have a notably light direct-service load, as measured in client contacts.

Pursuing this small lead, Mark eventually unearthed a stubborn artifact of the old culture, thriving in the midst of his change. Under several former directors, staff had been expected to protect managers from direct client contact as much as possible. For a variety of reasons, this protective behavior was continuing. As a result, clients were getting stuck on service plateaus with staff who were short of the knowledge or authority to help, despite their earnest desires and attempts to do so—staff who were working hard trying to solve sticky budgetary problems without bothering their bosses.

Now Mark had a decision to make. Was this behavior just a small glitch in the current change effort, one that he could correct with an agency-wide memo? Or was it an opening into the next Change Cycle, one that would reform this agency's entire way of thinking about and delivering client services?

Mark and his team decided on the latter course. Their review of the past year's accomplishments inspired new ideas of what was possible in this agency: that a group of competent, internally focused accountants could become effective client-centered financial consultants to their client agencies. On occasion even now, one of them would suggest a plan to serve a particular client in a new way, usually in response to a problem of long standing in the client agency. The team was pretty sure that the time was coming—not too far away now—when they could be involved in developing some entirely new concepts of service. Mark concurred, and imagined his agency becoming a model of exemplary client service, enabling all of its client agencies as well.

Mark put his immediate problem with appropriate referrals aside for a few days as he watched the changes take hold. As soon as he felt comfortable with the level of everyone's ability and cooperation, he was ready to move on. But first, he took care to share office-wide his assessment of just how much they all had learned and accomplished so far, and his confidence that they were nearing the target set over a year ago.

Then, because he had clients with real and immediate problems to solve, he rolled into Stage Seven—acknowledging the agency's accomplishments, and setting the stage for a new cycle of change that would bring about a greater sense of teamwork among staff and managers and successful collaborations with clients.

The time Mark spent in Stage Six, "Consolidating the Learning", secured the changes he and his staff had worked so hard to complete, and freed them to move forward. Days later, reviewing their measurable progress, Mark and his staff were able to celebrate that this change effort had finally hit the mark, and to look forward with confidence to the challenges to come.

Without the benefit of Stage Six reflections, the future will remain murkier than need be. You aren't necessarily clear where you stand now that the change has been made, and it's certainly unclear where you want to go next. Since there is no clear understanding of the extent and limits of the change that has been accomplished, it is unclear what remains to be done and what new possibilities have truly opened up because of the new situation. Limitations aren't identified and addressed. New possibilities and potential are neither identified nor exploited. In order to get the most benefit from the work you've done and to assure continuity from this Change Cycle to the next, the reflection of Stage Six must take place.

Recognize Your Accomplishments and Prepare for Transition: Stage Seven

The only work to do at Stage Seven, "Moving to the Next Cycle", is to recognize that you're there, and stimulate movement to the next cycle. Take full advantage of the transitional period to look back with a sense of satisfaction upon what has been accomplished, and to look forward to what you wish to do next. The potential barrier is that you may get stuck on the cusp between two cycles of change. To overcome that barrier, the role of the change leaders is to create enough felt need, enthusiasm, and momentum at the closure of the present cycle to transition successfully to the next. Discomfort with unresolved issues or new ones often serves as a powerful stimulus at this stage.

Without acknowledging your arrival at this point in the process, you may not pause to enjoy what has already been accomplished, and you may not realize that the next cycle is potentially at hand. Whether you or your group choose to move on to another cycle of change is up to you, but understanding your location in the change process makes that choice clear.

I believe, however, that our natural impulse is to move forward, from one cycle of change to the next. Certainly we may choose periods of rest between cycles. But to deny this impulse to continuously improve is to deny a primordial driving force within us all.

SECTION II

Approaches to Managing Change

Chapter 4
Special Issues in Managing Change Cycles

The Change Cycle management issues and examples we've explored so far have dealt mainly with change in organizational systems, processes, and behaviors. The Change Cycle model and the principles of change are equally applicable to other organizational issues. This chapter discusses some other applications of these concepts and presents usage observations and practical suggestions. The suggestions have been distilled from my management and consulting experience, and represent a selection of the most helpful Change Cycle management ideas I have seen. These principles can help people respond constructively to all kinds of problems.

Leadership: Visionary, Catalyst, Sustaining Force

Understanding the Change Cycle can be helpful in implementing change, but understanding isn't enough. One ingredient in the mix that must not be overlooked is leadership. Whether we are dealing with the ability to lead others or oneself, it is difficult to imagine change occurring without a leader. The leader supplies many of the elements necessary to enable change.

Leaders usually shape a vision or clearly define the target to build potential for change. They most often provide the initial thrust to get things started, and may be required to supply the sustaining drive needed to overcome barriers along the way.

Sometimes a leader must have the will to sustain a change effort despite great obstacles. Regardless of any doubts about self or about the value of the change, the effective leader of change must be able to instill enough motivation in others to drive the process through its inevitable obstacles. Moreover, an effective leader often supplies many of the motivational and at least some of the instrumental capabilities needed to move a change effort forward.

In practice, most change is not initiated by the will of many individuals who share a common purpose and vision. More often, change begins in the mind of a single person. For the motivation to spread to others, some kind of persuasive communication must occur between the originator of the idea and others. Without this communication, the change process can't spread beyond its originator.

This can occur in many ways and at any point during the originator's own processing of the change. As a leader, you must communicate ideas so that others are stimulated to want the change as well. This ability to be a catalytic agent for change, whether at the beginning of a change process or later on, is an invaluable asset for a leader.

Two roles that may fall upon the leader have been discussed: originator of the vision for change and catalyst to stimulate others. Let's look at a third role in more detail—that of sustaining force driving the change process through to completion. In many instances, other people will not see the value of a change until it is apparent and the effects of the change can be viewed directly. In order for the change process to run its course in these cases, someone who does see the value of the change must supply the driving force until others can appreciate its potential.

As the leader of the effort, you may have an inner struggle about whether this change is the right one, or whether this is the right time or the right way to pursue it. But if you flinch before others are ready to supply the motivating force for change, the effort will die. It isn't enough for you to provide the vision and be the initial catalyst for change. Unless or until others take up the banner, you must provide the driving force. You may even need to sustain this effort throughout the Change Cycle until the change has become an ongoing part of people's lives.

In summary, three leadership roles or functions are fundamental to activate and drive the change process: visionary, catalyst, and sustaining force. These are all roles that can be filled as needed. The profile of an effective leader would include these essential capabilities combined with others, including creativity and intuition.

Leadership: Creativity and Intuition

How effective can a leader be without creative and intuitive skills? Nearly everyone would agree that these are valuable capabilities to possess, but how necessary are they? This depends on your perspective on the uniqueness of events. If each set of circumstances is sufficiently different from every other one, then no set formula, model, or technique will supply all the guidance needed to manage the situation. It is my contention that there is enough uniqueness in each situation to demand special attention that goes beyond the scope of any formula-bound or cookbook approach. There will always be some factors that are far more or far less important than could be accounted for in the formula, or there may be additional factors present not accounted for in the model. There is also a unique mix of people involved in any multi-person change process. Each person has his or her own particular personality and skills, and the interactive patterns between people will also be unique.

It is not that formulas and analysis cannot be extremely valuable; it is only that reliance upon them without recognition of their limitations can be ineffective and may consume a great deal of time and effort. In order to effectively manage change, all the available capability must be brought to bear on the process.

The ability to deal with each situation's uniqueness and to find the best solutions to fit the specific conditions at hand is largely dependent on the leader's judgment, intuitive understanding, and creativity. These capabilities are closely related and, for our purposes, will be considered as a single group. Without these capabilities, you would have to rely upon incomplete data bases and analytical techniques that could not really supply you with the answers you need for managing change.

When analytic pieces of a puzzle are mentally assembled into a picture of the whole, there is a creative, intuitive process operating. When conclusions are drawn, or solutions to knotty problems found, these same nonanalytical capabilities have been used. For you to be effective as a leader, you will probably have to draw some of your own conclusions and provide at least some solutions to practical problems. Others may do this as well, but chances are that as a leader you will be required to use your own intuitive and creative faculties along the way. The topic of intuition and how to access it is taken up in greater detail in Chapter Eight. For now, it may be helpful to keep in mind that the whole change process truly depends upon the use of all our talents, including intuition.

Organizational Definition

Organizational definition—that is, what an organization chooses as its purpose, scope, products or services, markets, and strategies—deserves special mention. Often people become so wrapped up in day-to-day tasks and operational problems that they lose sight of larger issues. By periodically stepping back and focusing directly on these larger organizational issues, dramatic changes can be set in motion.

Periodically doesn't mean every six months, but it may mean every year or two, depending on how swiftly things are changing within your organization or in the surrounding environment. If your industry, markets, or related technologies move swiftly, you may have to monitor these strategic issues more frequently. In most organizations, it makes sense to ask these larger strategic questions every couple of years. A great deal depends on the answers.

Most of what happens in an organization stems from and revolves around questions of organizational definition, whether or not the definition is articulated. What is our mission, and what are we trying to accomplish? What business are we in? What markets do we serve—or wish to serve? What do our customers need? What is our competition up to? What new capabilities must we develop in light of the answers to these questions? This isn't an exhaustive list, but you can see the wide range of issues that could be considered.

In grappling with the scope and direction of your organization, you will inevitably encounter limitations caused by the way your organization is designed to meet its goals and challenges. You will identify weaknesses that you wish to bolster, or whole new arenas you wish to enter. You may discover that the organization's current efforts are largely directed at the wrong targets, or that much wheel-spinning is occurring because the organization's direction isn't clear to enough people.

Your organization's resources can be more easily deployed toward relevant objectives once the desired scope, purpose, and direction of the organization is clearly defined. This definition will also make it easier to identify the best targets for change. The highest leverage areas for change could be anywhere, from the underlying systems of the organization to the kind of people who are needed for basic tasks. The need for change may arise in many different arenas of the organization or just one.

Recognizing Future Potential: Driving Force for Change

Almost invariably, there will be a significant gap between the way you want the organization to be and the way it is. This gap, once it is defined precisely and the future potential is recognized, can produce all the driving force needed to launch a Change Cycle. The change may be dramatic and far-reaching in its implications, or it may be the next logical step in a process of continuous, incremental improvement. Whatever the case, once the desire for change is present, the Change Cycle can begin in earnest.

Starting any process of change takes courage. You will need the ability to look evenly at your organization's shortcomings, at what is, in comparison with what you want or what is possible. It takes courage, frankly, because what you see in the present may be painful. But this pain can become the driving force for change. This assessment of your current state can represent the first step toward future improvement. The courage simply to begin the process is a decision for health rather than stagnation. It means trying to take control of your situation, rather than letting the inherent flux of the world dominate the way change occurs. Just getting started is something worth celebrating.

Whether we are affected by the world economic or political climate, technological advancements, shifting market demands, or other contemporary conditions, flux is constant in the environmental context of our endeavors. To step back and look at the whole picture is to begin the exercise of our will toward creating the desired change. Once we recognize a significant gap between where we are and where we would like to be, a strong motivation to bridge that gap is born. The seed for change has been planted.

Imperative Prerequisites for Change

There are several critical prerequisites for successful change efforts that should be reemphasized here:

1. Early and continuous top management understanding, commitment, approval, and involvement are essential if any change process is to succeed.
2. A high degree of trust between levels of the organization greatly facilitates any *participative* change process. If it doesn't already exist, establishing trust becomes a Change Cycle in itself, preliminary to any other contemplated changes. Building trust is neither easy nor an overnight process. Trust is hard to build and easy to destroy.
3. Expect significant change to take time, probably considerably more than was originally anticipated. There are no shortcuts to making effective, permanent organizational change. People require time and repeated opportunities to think about, talk about, try out, and struggle with significant change. Taking whatever time is required for this internal and interpersonal processing of the change is a critical factor.

Committing to Change

Never underestimate the degree of commitment—personal or organizational—needed to drive each and every stage of the change process. At any point, a shortage of this driving motivational force will cause the process to stall, or sometimes even to reverse. This implies a need for continuous monitoring in order to spot any breakdown—or even cracks—in the forces driving your change. Whether it is insufficient drive in key people, wavering belief because of implementation problems, slowness in obtaining the desired results, or flagging top management support, any shift in the level of commitment will be a serious hazard to the forward movement of change.

Within corporations, people are constantly trying to read the level of upper-management commitment to many things. If the organization is involved in a change effort, employees will be hypersensitive to any signs of waning commitment. Sometimes the organization may have difficulty reading top management's real intentions.

Example: Unintentional Mixed Messages

A nation-wide chain of restaurants recently instituted a large-scale Total Quality program. The program apparently had plenty of top-down support. The president personally presented his vision for the company's future to employees across the country, emphasizing the importance of Total Quality as the primary means for achieving this vision. The president and the regional general managers who reported directly to him were overseeing the entire process.

Formally, the Total Quality program showed up among the president's top five priorities for the company. In practice, however, the organization began to get mixed messages. Whenever short-term urgent issues arose, people would get pulled from the Total Quality project to respond. After several instances of redirected resources, the organization began to get a message that was contrary to the one the president wanted to send. If this unspoken message were put into words, it might read something like this:

In order to make this company work, we must continually focus attention on the most critical issues of the moment. When these issues come up, they take precedence over any other initiatives you may be working on. Yes, I believe in our long-term efforts to create a better company in the future. But if we don't give greater attention to these significant short-term issues, there will be no company left to build a future on.

In essence, he was unintentionally letting the organization know that responding to short-term problems was a "must do", while the longer-term change effort—Total Quality—was nice to do.

Managers of any change process must be continually aware of the messages—conscious and unconscious—they are sending regarding organizational commitment to a change process. The question here is not whether the president's emphasis on solving short-term problems is correct or not, but only to point out the impact it has on the Total Quality initiative. Another way to deal with the same situation might be to develop better methods of addressing emergency situations as part of the Total Quality program.

Along with monitoring change comes the need to assess the meaning and implications of real shifts in commitment. Is the shift significant? How far-reaching is it? Is it temporary or permanent? Can you do anything about it or not? Depending on the answers to these and similar questions, there may be a need for corrective action. But most important, be aware of the need for this continuous monitoring and feedback function with respect to commitment through the early and middle stages of the change process. The same functions are needed for other aspects of the change process, as well. I am emphasizing the need to pay attention to commitment level because people often do not pay enough attention to the ebb and flow of this driving motivational force, without which there can be no real change.

Communication Is Vital

Imagine that you are putting together a very complex puzzle. It is composed of many irregularly shaped pieces. The pieces themselves are made of various materials such as metal, plastic, ceramics, and wood. In order to fit this puzzle together you must apply glue, not just one type of glue, but several different kinds. Since you have never tried to glue some of these materials together, you might even have to experiment with different glues and methods of application.

Communication is the glue of organizational change. It must be applied liberally, at all stages of the process, and in a variety of ways. If there is not enough glue, or the wrong kind is used in the wrong place, the pieces won't all fit together.

In practice, it is important to give people a variety of repeated opportunities to become involved and to talk about the change process. People need to phrase, rephrase, paraphrase, again and again, what they are involved with and what it means to them. There are no shortcuts to this communication process. People are not machines with interchangeable parts. Taking time for this communication, probably considerably more than was originally anticipated, is an essential component in achieving permanent organizational change.

No Surprises

During the whole Change Cycle, communication provides a vital link among all interested parties. If more than one person is involved, information must flow freely: updates of all sorts, early warning systems, commitment checks, audit and feedback of progress and results, and information on course changes. Beyond these communication vehicles and the everyday functions they serve stands another significant principle: no surprises.

Surprises can be disastrous to anyone involved in the effort, including outside supporters and other interested parties. Even if an unexpected development has a beneficial effect, those who are surprised by the occurrence may react negatively. If the unanticipated event impedes progress in any way, the surprised parties will almost certainly respond negatively. Responses are often emotional, as if there has been a personal affront. People may express valid rational objections to what has occurred, but at base, you can expect to find feelings of having been let down

or left out of the primary feedback loop, or of not being highly
valued. This is true even among senior managers who know the
good reasons for controlling information flow and the difficulties
of keeping everyone informed. While these feelings can arise
whenever someone is left in a relative information vacuum, this
tendency is greatly exacerbated when there is a significant,
unexpected turn of events.

If you must err in terms of keeping people informed about a
change process, especially regarding significant events, then too
much information is better than too little. There is some vulnerability here, for example, when an organization is developing a
product for a customer and must report a slowdown that pushes
back the completion date. Despite this vulnerability, as a general
rule it's better to keep interested parties well informed so that
they can take in and process the significance of events
and plan accordingly.

Because of the importance of this "no surprises" idea, many
successful change efforts have used it as an operating principle
to guide behavior and to manage the expectations of all parties
throughout the cycle.

Act Quickly to Remedy Problems

Problems can develop quickly during a change process, and
demand swift, decisive action. I'm referring here to addressing
any significant breakdowns, gaps, shortcomings, or new factors
discovered through the monitoring of the change process. Let's
assume that you're reasonably sure of your data, and have spent
enough (just enough) time analyzing the situation so that you
know what corrective action is needed. Often the analysis and
action planning goes on far too long, and the window of
opportunity to make the required intervention closes. This is a
common occurrence, especially in complex organizations, but it
also occurs for individuals trying to make personal changes.

In managing the change process, it is much more common to
err on the side of caution, timidity, and extensive analysis than
on the side of bold, decisive action. Remember that as long as the
motivational forces remain intact, one can always make a mistake

and try again. There is certainly plenty of room for tactical errors and regrouping, but the strategic error of letting a significant problem go unchecked can quickly derail a change effort.

Allowing Appropriate Time for Change

Whenever people discuss implementing a change, an inevitable question follows: How long will it take to complete this change and realize the benefits? To fully imagine the desired new state means being willing to see the shortcomings and weaknesses of the present condition. Having seen the gap between the current state of affairs and the desired future state, the natural impulse is to bridge the gap—instantly. Tension inherent in seeing current limitations compared to future potential serves a practical purpose: it adds a sense of urgency and vitality to the change process.

However, the basic question remains. How can you make the change process move faster? Do some types of change typically occur faster than others? There are certain types of change that are inherently slow, and that have one thing in common: they require complex implementation processes. It is not so much the complexity of the issue itself, but the complexity of implementation once a solution has been found.

Suppose you have already found a universal vaccine for preventing cancer. Furthermore, assume that it is a simple matter to administer the vaccine, once a person agrees to the procedure and is physically present for the injection. The change from a cancer-prone population to a protected population now depends on an implementation process involving governmental testing and approval of the new medication, large-scale production, education of health care professionals, communication to a vast number of potential recipients, a large-scale distribution and services delivery system, and funding for the whole project. The Change Cycle cannot be completed quickly simply because of the practical complexities inherent in the solution. While the benefits for people, not to mention the profit potential to the manufacturer, will provide strong motivations, time will be needed to create the system that produces and delivers this vaccine.

The reason for the complexity can vary a great deal. For example, changing an organization's culture is complex because it requires changing people's attitudes as well as their behaviors. Sometimes a cultural shift must be accomplished through shifting the attitudes of people one person at a time. Even when many people can rapidly shift the way they think about something, such as their jobs or their company, it may take a long time for the practical structures, systems, and behavior patterns to catch up to their new values, attitudes, or beliefs.

Example: Time Needed for Complex Change

Think of the dramatic changes that have taken place in the Swiss watchmaking industry since the advent of quartz technology. Prior to the widespread sales of Japanese watches using quartz movements, the Swiss had always thought of the watchmaking business in terms of refinements in mechanical movements. Their whole outlook on their industry, markets, technical development, competition, skills, and their own future was based on a paradigm revolving around mechanical watch technology.

When quartz movements seriously eroded their markets, the Swiss began to rethink their entire outlook on watchmaking. Their attitudes toward the viability and potential impact of non-mechanical watch technology first had to shift radically. Then the practical structures of their business had to change as they started up new electronic watch divisions and factories, and diversified their product lines. Whole new corporate structures emerged, and a dramatic reshuffling of organizational priorities occurred.

At the systems level, changes included new manufacturing systems, technical support systems, and computerized quality control. Low-cost manufacturing techniques replaced or supplemented handcrafting. At the behavioral level, fewer people were needed to perform the old watchmaking functions, while more people were needed to design and build electronic mechanisms. In addition, the whole image of the Swiss industry had to be reshaped and entirely new approaches to marketing developed.

A very complex set of changes, indeed. No wonder it has taken so long for the Swiss to respond to the Japanese challenge.

Example: Less Obvious Complexities

Sometimes it isn't obvious that complexities exist. While people may be well aware of behaviors that will need to change, they are less aware of the shifts needed in attitudes. This was the case in a large corporation that wanted to centralize its accounting functions. The corporation was made up of more than a dozen relatively independent divisions. Each was considered to be a separate business unit that would stand or fall based on its own profitability. Management had identified certain functions that could be made more efficient by centralizing resources and consolidating corporate expertise. Accounting was one such area.

The benefits of centralization were envisioned as sizable reductions in duplication of functions, simplification of accounting and tax procedures, reduction of resource requirements, and fewer mistakes and less confusion. But there would also be a significant increase in how much the central office would know about each of its business units. Under the new accounting system, each of the independent business units would find it much harder to control critical information about costs, revenues, and business trends. Each business unit would be subject to more frequent and more precise examination by corporate headquarters. This closer corporate scrutiny led to perceptions of not being trusted and to fears that corporate management was trying to exercise greater control over how each business was run. Regardless of the true intentions behind the new accounting system, these feelings of mistrust and suspicions of upper management's motives represented a major barrier to implementation.

The significance of this barrier was multiplied because these business units were spread out geographically and each was unique in terms of internal dynamics. Some businesses had a steady stream of revenue that could be accurately represented on a month-to-month basis. Other businesses received payments sporadically for products or services. Monthly or even quarterly reporting could be very misleading. The problem became one of creating a single accounting system that accurately represented the ongoing financial health of each of these unique businesses.

The real complexity in making a system change across these business units was not found in the uniqueness of their businesses, but in their people. What upper management wanted was a more efficient accounting system that gave them better information on the current state of each business. There was no desire on the part of upper management to change the values and attitudes of all these people. All that was desired was better status information on a more timely basis, with fewer associated expenses. Regardless of management's real motives, there was resistance in the business units to the accounting system changes due to mistrust and the desire for independence. Whether management liked it or not, employee attitudes needed to be changed in order to accomplish what seemed a relatively straightforward change in systems and related behavior.

If human factors in the change process are ignored, problems will likely arise. Changes in behavior more often than not also involve changes in attitudes. As soon as the question of how to change people's attitudes enters the picture, a whole new level of complexity is introduced into the implementation process. No longer are we dealing with simple shifts in the way people do things; we must also deal with fundamental ways in which the activity itself is viewed. Changing people's perspectives on an activity is no simple matter, and may involve great time and effort. Many times the only approach that works is a person-by-person persuasion campaign, and even this must often be backed up by proof of corporate intentions.

Example: A Simpler Change

In contrast, consider a far simpler change in a work setting: switching telephone systems. Despite all the technical setup and linkage problems, and despite all the retraining necessary to take advantage of the new system's capabilities, there is a high likelihood that people will adjust quickly. Certain behavior changes will be required to effectively use the new system. Conference calls may be easier to set up, but a new technique must be mastered first. Similarly, it may be possible to manage a larger stream of incoming calls once certain routing functions are changed.

Except in cases where using the new capabilities of the phone system dramatically affect the nature of one's job, the installation of the new system will not represent a major change in people's lives. They needn't shift their attitudes toward their jobs, or their view of themselves. There is no wrestling with knotty questions about priorities or values. One need only learn a few new techniques and shift some phone usage habits to extract value from the new system. Now, in practice, implementing a new phone system may be a lot more complex and time consuming than it appears to be on the surface. But it will never compare in complexity to implementing a change that involves shifting people's attitudes as well as their behaviors.

Methods to Speed Up a Change Process

So far, then, we have been looking at examples of how the complexity of implementation has a dramatic impact on the speed of change. Whether the scale of change is large or small, the speed of change is dominated by this factor. This is not to say other factors are not at work as well, only that once the desired change has been isolated, practical implementation difficulties are the primary consideration. This leads to our next point.

Much can be done to speed up a change process once the resolution has been identified. Speeding up the process can be a matter of raising its level of priority, bolstering resource allocations, or removing barriers wherever feasible. It is quite possible to focus a great deal of attention on the change effort, and to sustain that attention for as long as is required. It may mean that key people spend all their time working with others to implement the change. It may mean that the CEO is out on the shop floor not just talking to people about the importance of making the change, but working with them on actual implementation.

Speeding up the change process by these means amounts to

an application of will demonstrated to an organization by the persistent focus, unusual level of effort, deployment of resources, and intensity of tone. If these demonstrations are not enough to speed things along, then something else is missing. Perhaps the individual or organization attempting to make the change lacks some critical capability. On the other hand, the problem may lie in the type of change that is being attempted.

Gauging the Needed Effort

There are many situations in which implementation of change is complex and the process will probably extend over months, at least. In these cases, there is the need to keep assessing when and how hard to push for change. Only through sensitivity to the specific conditions at hand can one determine just when and how hard to push for speeding up the process.

If one pushes too hard, there is always the danger of creating greater resistance to the change. Pushing too hard when people are already putting forth their best efforts raises the risk of deflating enthusiasm and slowing the momentum for change. In these cases, it is more important to let the process play out than to push for greater speed. On the other hand, if a real opportunity exists to speed things along and the demands for the change are great enough, there may be every reason to push. It is truly a judgment call, but judgment is always enhanced by knowledge of the possible consequences.

Don't Underestimate the Time and Effort
Needed for Change

We all know that change is difficult, but we still tend to grossly underestimate the time, effort, and conscious attention needed to accomplish a desired change. We tend to fool ourselves into believing that the change process is complete, when it is really in mid-course. We tend to underestimate the barriers we will face along the way, as well as the tenacity of existing values and behavior patterns. It is not enough to plan for these difficulties ahead of time, in the initial stages of the Change Cycle. It is necessary to continually be on guard against misjudging how far you have come, how pervasive and deeply rooted is the resistance to change, or how many people have truly adapted the new pattern.

It is useful to have a model and a few reference points along the way to help keep track of progress toward your goals. Reminders of typical problems and effective responses can also be useful. This is where the description of the Change Cycle can help. By referring to it on an ongoing basis, it will be much easier to determine where you are in the process, what typical issues you may be facing next, and maybe even to get some ideas on how to solve those problems. This model is valid for a wide variety of situations, yet can be tailored to suit your specific purposes.

Two Key Factors: Motivation and Capability

Sometimes it helps to apply the simplest, most straightforward tests to your change effort. One such test is to boil all the key factors down to two: motivation and capability. Does your organization have enough motivation toward the change to drive through the process and address all the problems you will face along the way? Does your organization have the skills and resources necessary to develop the plans, address implementation problems, and actually perform well with the change in place? If not, what can you do to increase the level of motivation and skills?

There is a direct question that can help you determine whether you have a motivation or a skill-based problem: If people absolutely had to make the change, could they do it? If the answer is "yes", you are likely dealing with a motivation issue. If the answer is "no", then there is probably a lack of capability present. In my experience, the answer to this question usually points to insufficient motivation. It seems to be easier to build or obtain capability than it is to build and sustain motivation. That is why I place so much emphasis on building commitment.

Flexibility

As a Change Cycle moves along, unexpected twists and turns appear in the road. The need to adjust your plans and expectations, sometimes substantially, is part of the process. This need to adapt is not only a matter of adjusting to difficulties. Sometimes golden opportunities arise and are missed because of an unwillingness or inability to shift course.

Example: Be Prepared to Change Course

Within a large industrial corporation, a research and development team has taken on a product design project for one of their corporate division clients. Their task is to design a new microcomputer-based sensing and recording device for in-plant quality control of the chemical manufacturing process. The device will provide ongoing readouts as well as data storage capability for key quality control data. Specifically, the device will be used to precisely monitor the mix of ingredients and to flag any deviations from the optimum mixture. It will be a stand-alone unit designed to interface with automatic mixture control devices on various brands of factory equipment.

The design team, mainly from the corporate R&D department, has been working on this device for several months now, and is excited about its potential. Here is a rather straightforward design project that could well result in a successful entry into the marketplace, industry-wide recognition for the company as a technological leader in its field, and internal recognition of the R&D department as a valuable contributor to corporate success.

It has become clear, however, that the stand-alone unit may be only one application of this technology. The divisional client who has contracted with R&D to design the stand-alone unit has begun to shift its interest in another direction. They now recognize that there is greater potential for this device if it could be fully integrated with the company's own products. A subsystem could be designed that would not only monitor the chemical mix, but automatically regulate the flow of ingredients. This could represent a technological edge for their own machinery, compared to the competition's products. Why give this competitive edge away? Why not develop an integrated subsystem for their own products, and let the competition try to catch up?

The only problem is that the design team has already done a

great deal of work on the stand-alone unit, and many design parameters would have to be completely reworked to produce a dedicated, fully integrated subsystem. This would not be a simple modification of the design specifications, it would be an entirely new project. Furthermore, the divisional client (primarily a manufacturing organization) wants to simply change the design specifications and continue on the existing contract with R&D. They argue that much of the same technology and design work that was already completed could be easily adapted to the proposed dedicated unit. Not only does the divisional client want this, but upper management is intrigued with this notion of the dedicated subsystem.

R&D had everyone putting pressure on them to radically reorganize their design work. Yet no one seemed to understand how difficult it would be to make this shift, or how much time and effort would be discarded. They were expected to simply respond to the new demand, and eat the extra cost. Of course, they would still be held to their original time and financial objectives!

Our purpose is not to judge who was right or what is fair. From our consideration of the change process, what has occurred in this situation happens frequently. People learn as they go along. No one recognized the real competitive opportunity of a dedicated subsystem until the design project was well underway. And so, as it became clear that this new product feature had greater potential for the organization than the original application, a radical shift seemed appropriate. Now, given unlimited budgets and technical resources, it might be possible to pursue both products simultaneously, but this is rarely the case. In some cases it might make more sense to finish the first product before pursuing the new one. Early recognition that such shifts could occur also suggests a need for closer, more frequent contact with the division customer. This way, less investment would be made in one solution before there were signals that a change in direction is warranted.

But the point here is that many times the burden to shift course in midstream falls squarely on those most intimately involved with making the change. It is better to recognize this as a real possibility in advance and be prepared with contingency plans than to be caught by surprise.

Managing Shifts in Ownership

During change efforts involving groups of people, there is often an intentional shift in ownership and even in leadership that must occur during the process in order for successful completion to occur. This shift may occur as a project moves from the design phase to the implementation phase (as was the case in the example of Rob's new computer-assisted project management system in Chapter Three), or it may occur at any other point in the cycle. If the ownership and resulting change in leadership of the effort slips at this point—perhaps due to incomplete transference or simply not understanding who must take ownership—then further movement through the change process is seriously jeopardized.

It is rare that significant, lasting change happens when ownership and/or leadership evaporates. Without it, sustained effort in the desired direction will almost certainly cease. It is fairly easy to identify points in an ongoing effort where shifts in leadership or ownership by principal participants must occur. If a change effort is being monitored with this "shift of ownership" possibility in mind, it is a simple matter to recognize. However, major changes in who leads an effort or who must feel ownership require substantial care and effort.

Again, the example of the operations support system (Chapter Three, as above) comes to mind. Notice how much careful effort went into orienting and training operational personnel prior to implementation, and still it was not enough. The key to making such transitions work is recognizing when each and every one of the people who needs to feel ownership has made a personal shift in their commitment. This is not a matter of applying a set formula to the orientation and training of people, but rather of doing whatever it takes to encourage the shift in their perspective.

Straightening the Pathway to Change

Change motivated by strong desire has movement and life of its own. Even if we were to try to stop a desire-driven, consciously directed change from occurring, we couldn't. We can do a great deal to facilitate or inhibit progress, but when a person or group wants change badly enough, events will usually move in the desired direction. It may not be a smooth or efficient pathway, but directional, nonetheless. Individual or collective will sustains movement.

How do you increase the strength, vitality, and life-span of an organization? One way is to start by identifying a worthwhile change that most people already recognize as valuable. Learn by studying and discussing the Change Cycle and identifying how effectively change has occurred within your organization in the past. Try to pinpoint major driving forces and restraining forces in your organization that could impact this particular change. Then plot an entire Change Cycle for achieving the change you've selected.

Anticipate hurdles and barriers at each stage of the cycle, and plan how you might overcome them. Don't spend too much time in this planning mode—just enough to be sure you've identified a good target. Along the way, check whether you continue to feel that the results are worth the effort, and that you have a real chance to pull it off.

You can launch your effort without a set of precise goals, but at a minimum you will need a directional target with recognized potential. You also must have enough confidence in your capability to overcome the inevitable obstacles along the way. By all means, once these criteria are met, get moving. Don't linger too long in the planning mode; make your initial commitment and give it your best shot. Trust your own judgment and your ability to come up with whatever solutions are needed to drive the whole process through to the end. You're entering an exhilarating process.

You must be willing to count on your own capabilities and those of others in your organization to solve whatever problems arise. When appropriate, use group problem solving to draw out the creativity of your colleagues. Models, tools, analysis, and experience are only part of the story. You must be willing to take some risk, and to trust your own intuitive powers to pull you through.

Understanding the seven stages of the Change Cycle and mastering techniques to manage the process is only a means to smoothing and straightening the pathway to change. With enough desire driving the process, the change will tend to be self-sustaining over time, eventually approaching the desired end state. But there may be unnecessary confusion, blind alleys, wasted energy, and frustration along the way. The ability to guide this process, to anticipate and effectively address problems as they arise, and to steadfastly exercise greater control over the internal dynamics of change, is an extremely valuable capability. This book has been written to help you build that capability.

Chapter 5
Imposed Change

Change can be made using many different methods. Some managers depend on the commitment of participants for implementing change successfully; others impose change on people against their will. In this chapter, I'll discuss change that is achieved by an individual or group by imposing one's will on others.

Whether or not well intentioned, imposed change occurs when an attempt is made to remove or confuse another's freedom of choice. The question considered here isn't whether this method is sometimes right or necessary, but whether it can work. Can change be accomplished in this way or not? What are the costs and by-products of imposed change that should be taken into account when deciding whether or not to use this method?

Three Questions to Ask Before Imposing Change

Managers and others routinely face choices about what methods to use in making change. When considering imposing change on others, three important factors are often overlooked or undervalued:

1. Will people choose to accept the change, to go along with it?
2. If not, should you force change, regardless of the level of resistance?
3. If you do force change, and the change is completed, will people value its benefits?

These factors are relevant in any situation in which the driving force for change is external to those expected to make the change—that is, whenever they have not yet taken ownership or internalized belief in the change. By considering these questions as you contemplate any directed change process, you can better assess the difficulty of the task, and whether or not it makes sense to impose change on others. Each of these questions will be explored before we draw overall conclusions about the feasibility and possible consequences of imposing change.

Why Accept Imposed Change?

Why would anyone choose to go along with a change with which they don't agree? First, the change itself may not be important enough to resist. Second, people may feel obligated to comply, even if they disagree. This can occur because of an explicit or felt obligation to an employer or other authority. For example: "I have to do it. It's expected of me as part of my job." Third, people may accept imposed change if superordinate values drive their decision, as when a person believes in a cause and chooses to accommodate leadership decisions with which he or she doesn't agree in order to advance that cause.

The fourth reason for choosing to accede to an externally driven change is that the change represents the lesser of two evils. The choice may be perceived as going along with an unwanted change versus facing an even worse consequence. Driving the choice in the latter case could be an expressed or implied threat for noncompliance. There are many historical precedents for choosing to go along with laws or ordinances rather than risk reprisal. There are also precedents for noncompliance, despite the consequences.

Why Force Change?

If people don't have reason to cooperate with change they disagree with, will you force the change against their will? Forced change has many faces, spanning the spectrum from overtly hostile—such as one country imposing its will on another through military force—to subtle, as when a subordinate is expected to carry out a corporate directive despite his own feelings or beliefs. Parents may require obedience from their young children despite all protests. Whether or not forced change can endure once the external force is removed will be discussed later.

Without a doubt, it's possible to force change. When people are forced to change in important ways, however, there are inevitable by-products. These aren't pleasant to contemplate. People begin to doubt their own power and effectiveness in managing the world around them. They may lose faith in others as well as themselves. They may begin to see negative motives in others, regardless of how pure their motives may be.

Coerced people feel angry and frustrated. These emotions will likely stay alive for the duration of the change process, and may be expressed against both the change and the one(s) imposing it. Negative feelings engendered by being forced usually endure beyond completion of the change. People literally can have their whole outlook on life and their belief in themselves altered. These by-products of being forced to comply with someone else's wishes are worth careful consideration before you decide to impose change, especially when people both disagree with the change and lack other motives to cooperate.

Delayed Recognition of the Value of Change

The real value and potential of some changes are difficult to imagine in advance. Many changes must be complete for the benefits to be seen and appreciated. Will people recognize the value of the change once it's completed? Will the end justify the means? People's judgment of a change can alter dramatically once the change is complete, or when they can view the change and change process from a new perspective.

Here's an example: For five years, employees in a federal environmental agency had used a simple electronic mail system to link their ten departments and branch offices together. Then management decided to upgrade to a more sophisticated e-mail program that could better serve their growing agency's needs. Announcements of the impending switch to the new program were made, and employees were encouraged to attend training sessions on using the new e-mail system software.

On the announced date, the information services group installed the new e-mail program on the agency's computer network. When the employees returned to work the following day, there were many complaints. Some people, who were quite computer literate and enjoyed playing with new software, easily made the switch to the new e-mail program. Others had considerable difficulty. Most of the staff were quite busy, and getting used to a new program was one more demand to cram into an already overflowing schedule. Most of the employees felt that the old e-mail was sufficient, and that this new program was both an unnecessary expense for the agency and a pain to learn. Staff resentment of this imposed change fueled people's criticisms of the new system.

As many important messages were sent by e-mail in this office, people had no choice but to use the new system. They could not go about their typical early morning routines of reading and sending mail without adjusting to the new program. Complaints continued among those who resisted learning how to use the new software. However, over time, the virtues of the new e-mail system became apparent even to the complainers. It facilitated communication between the main office and outlying branches. Many more options were available to forward messages, to send messages to a group, and so forth. Even those who had resisted learning the system became comfortable using it and really did appreciate its flexibility and greater range of choices. After they experienced the benefits of the new system, the value of the change was recognized.

Similarly, people can look back on forced changes in their lives and see value both in the results and the process. Perception of the actual value—or even of the intended value—of results can dramatically shift how we view a change process. Whether people choose to go along with a change they don't believe in or they are forced to comply, they may later value the change and even the process used, if the benefits become recognized and important to them.

Difficulties Caused by Imposing Change: An Example

An example from the workplace may help here. Suppose that the leadership of an organization activates a major change in its inventory control system. Management believes that the new system will not only save time, effort, and money, but it will cut down on shipment errors as well. A few upper-level managers see the potential of the change, and impose the new system in all of the company's warehouses.

The warehouse employees have their doubts. At first they grumble about the system. Then they decide to actively resist it. Small acts of sabotage begin to occur in several of the warehouses. The culprits can't be identified; their co-workers protect them. For a time, it appears that costly breakdowns in the delivery system are going to threaten the whole company. At this point, upper management decides to deal with the problem swiftly and decisively. No union is involved, so without complication, management lets many warehouse employees go, hiring replacements. The new employees are trained to use the new inventory system. Presto—the change has been accomplished. Whether or not we believe in the method used, it has worked.

As an alternative, if management had pushed long and hard enough, opposition to the new system among the original employees might have dissipated. People might have chosen the lesser of two distasteful alternatives: use the new system or lose your job. Eventually, the new system would probably have become routine. However, in this example, management followed a more rapid and severe course: firing employees to avert an imminent threat to the business.

The example above illustrates several points about externally driven change. People can and do impose their will on others, and change can be accomplished in this way. This method can operate on a small or large scale, and it can work quickly. Sometimes it may appear to be the only practical way to get things done.

But recall that great difficulties can result with this approach. Practical problems can surface as you take steps to impose your will on others who don't share your commitment. Even if change occurs, without the commitment of those whose behaviors have shifted, can the change last?

Instability of Change Without Commitment

Commitment is a central factor in any change process; it implies desire focused on an objective. As we've discussed, the desire or driving force for change can come from outside, and may cause people to make changes against their wishes. But can real directional change come about in this way, or is acquiescence under these circumstances likely to be temporary? Under what conditions can forced change endure?

A few examples may help clarify matters. It is perfectly possible for people to reluctantly go along with a change that they oppose while waiting for the chance to rebel once the external driving forces are removed. Consider historically how often and how long religiously suppressed peoples have gone underground with their beliefs, waiting for the opportunity to express openly what they desire. Once the oppressive force of governmental restraint is removed, their behavior immediately reverts. Change in their religious behavior was manifest only so long as the outside driving force was sustained. No permanent shift had occurred within these people, only an accommodation to an oppressive external force.

In times of crisis, as well, outside force is ineffective in creating enduring change. People may make dramatic shifts in their behavior in times of great need. Exceptional acts of unselfishness and heroism exemplify our capabilities as humans. Nevertheless, once the crisis ends there is usually a return to former behavior patterns. Crisis-driven changes in behavior are not sustained because they aren't internally motivated. Once the driving force is removed, there is insufficient internal motivation to make the change a permanent part of self.

Sustained External Pressure Can Create Change

External driving forces are difficult, but not impossible, to sustain long enough to make an unwanted change stick. Let's return to the example of the new inventory control system. Assume that the benefits of the new system are real, but that these benefits can't be demonstrated convincingly until the system has been in full operation for a number of months. This might well lead to the warehouse employees resisting the change. After all, they would have to take someone else's word for the benefits, while dealing directly with all the practical difficulties of making the switch to a new way of doing their jobs.

Yet management is committed to this change. If management can sustain its emphasis on implementation and full use of the new system long enough, the workers may begin to recognize its benefits, and eventually to accept it. Their resistance may transform into commitment once the benefits become manifest.

The difficulty comes in trying to sustain outside pressure long enough for people to see how effective a new system might be. Most often, management's own commitment—or its ability to sustain sufficient driving force—will fade before the change has taken hold. If this happens, the change, no matter how potentially beneficial, won't become widespread and permanent.

When can you expect to be able to impose change successfully? While it is possible to cause change in this way, certain conditions must be present in order for it to work. For example, the change can become permanent if the potential or the benefits of the change are eventually recognized; people may embrace the change even though it was imposed.

There is a second set of circumstances where externally driven change will work, as well. If the external desire or will can sustain pressure for a long enough time, certain kinds of change may become part of the normal routine of life. This occurs when there is not enough benefit in resisting or reverting to the old pattern once the new way of doing things becomes the norm. The key to avoiding reversion to former patterns of behavior lies in the perceived potential or benefit of shifting back. When dealing with something people really care about—for example, their freedom or religious beliefs—a return to former desired patterns is likely once external pressure is removed. Only where the externally driven change isn't that important to people will they eventually accept it as part of their lives, even if given the choice to change back.

The permanence of externally driven change rests on two closely related factors. First, do people eventually recognize the value of the imposed change? If so, the internal commitment to change will shift, based on their experience and firsthand evidence. Second, is the old way of thinking and doing things so important that no amount of sustained external pressure will create an internal shift? In this case, if the internal commitment to the old idea or pattern remains high and constant, no permanent shift will occur. The implication is clear: one way or another, permanent change requires a shift in one's thinking.

To reiterate, the only exception occurs when a change isn't important enough to mobilize resistance or to motivate reversion to former behaviors. When not enough value is placed on the change, people won't make the effort to resist indefinitely or to change back to their earlier pattern.

Externally Imposed Change: An Example

To illustrate these points, it may help to look at an example from industry. In one manufacturing organization, the inconsistent daily flow of product through the assembly process had been an ongoing problem for years. Several competent plant managers had tried and failed to accomplish smooth production flow. Despite their efforts, nearly all finished product came off the assembly line at or close to the end of the month, resulting in a costly glut of effort compressed into a few days of the month and great spans of slack time during the rest of the month.

Then a new manager entered the scene, and things did change. Les Cahill had been schooled in a hard-nosed approach to management: define your goals, action plan, and measurement techniques; assign accountabilities; hold people's feet to the fire; and keep driving until the mission is accomplished. Les applied this approach to the production problem with intensity for well over a year. Not only was the smooth flow of production Les's major focus, it appeared to be his only focus. He became so wrapped up in solving this problem that it seemed to consume him. He spent nearly all of his time gathering updated information and pushing people to achieve the results he wanted. This went much further than simply asking for results. Les exerted pressure without much care for the emotional impact of his style. He was certainly feared, disliked, and mistrusted. His staff also expected (some would say hoped) that this job was merely a stopping-off point in Les's career. They felt used; Les couldn't be counted on to take care of them in the future.

Their contributions were rewarded formally by salary increases, promotions, and greater job security during down-sizing periods, but no one had a sense of personal relationship with or loyalty to Les. He rarely gave informal praise for good results. While Les was viewed as having great competence and drive, people felt he was cold and inflexible.

With little of his humanity showing, Les was able to accomplish what none of his predecessors had been able to do: he solved the production flow problem. Then, as expected, Les moved on as soon as the opportunity for a better position presented itself. But many of the changes remained intact, even without Les's presence at the plant. The overall change was completed. Why did this relatively unappealing method of imposing change work? After all, prior managers had tried similar methods, but changes didn't stick. Essentially, Les did what none of the others was willing to do— he overcame people's resistance to change by imposing his will. In this case, the change was enabled by Les's persistent drive.

During Les's tenure, new systems were put in place to identify the key points in the production process that influenced the flow from raw materials to finished product. The system gave early warning of potential trouble spots, so people could take corrective action as required. Tighter requirements for parts suppliers were enforced, resulting in fewer delays caused by late, missing, or unacceptable parts. Quality control checks were now made throughout the assembly process, instead of relying entirely on final product check-out. All expediter jobs, formerly critical to making it through the month-end scramble, were eliminated. These changes and others became routine while Les was in charge.

Although Les had forced these changes on the whole plant, his new systems and related procedures worked well. They not only smoothed out production, but made everyone's job more manageable. Despite residual bad feelings about Les and his methods, people did see the benefits of the new systems and continued to use them.

Changes Les made to nonoperational systems and procedures did not stick, however. The endless meetings and confrontations used to implement change were no longer needed. Neither was Les's confrontative, high-pressure style of management. Once Les was gone, the workers reverted to their preferred friendly, interactive relations. No one on the production line valued Les's methods of obtaining change, only his results.

However, managers in other parts of the company did attach value to Les's methods. They observed the positive results he had obtained and they certainly noticed his career flourishing. Les left behind a group of managers who, like him, saw the benefit of being less interested in their impact on people than on how their changes, once in place, might improve productivity, product quality, customer satisfaction, and profitability. They decided these factors would have a significant impact on the long-term viability of the organization, and they began to copy Les's methods. They may or may not have been rationalizing their true motives, but that's not the point.

Their expressed goals may have seemed worthy, but at what cost? It is a matter of choice and a matter of degree. The same goals could have been achieved without such human cost as part of the equation. There is no denying that such methods can be highly effective in obtaining change. This doesn't mean, however, that they are the only or the preferred means.

When to Consider Imposing Change

When considering whether to use methods of externally imposed change, examine your situation closely. Suppose that you're in charge and that your motives are clear. All you're looking for is the most practical and effective means of creating change.

You're simply trying to implement what you're convinced is a worthwhile improvement.

Should you choose an approach that depends upon many people in your organization supporting the improvement? Or should you use a direct mandate? You're convinced that either method can work, but it seems so much simpler, more direct, and quicker to order the change.

Start evaluating your options by considering the potential of the change you're trying to implement. Do you think that people will be able to recognize that potential just by hearing about it? Can you demonstrate the benefits before people experience the results through a completed Change Cycle? Is there some way for them to imagine the same end state that you can see, and to become excited about it, just as you are?

If the answer to any of these questions is "yes", then the change process can work well by building commitment, depending upon people's own will to drive the process. This isn't to suggest that it will be easy, only that it's quite feasible. If, on the other hand, your answers to these questions are "no", then you may wish to consider the mandate approach.

Note that some organizational cultures *expect* imposed change and, within limits, really do accept it. But before assuming that imposed change will readily be accepted, you need to be very familiar with an organization. If your assumption is wrong, imposing change can result in a drop in employee morale and effectiveness.

Mandating Change: Pros and Cons

You may run into great difficulty persuading people about the potential, the benefits, and the practical value of a given change prior to their seeing its effects in reality. When this is true, your next step is to examine your own convictions about the outcomes of this Change Cycle. Are you really convinced of the potential benefits? Can you visualize the changes working? Can you imagine, in considerable detail, people successfully doing things in the new way?

Are you ready to risk the side effects of the mandate approach, if you are unable to complete the Change Cycle? If the changes never manifest so that people can see their value, you'll have led them to a very uncomfortable dead end. You'll have mandated a change that never happened, and raised expectations about benefits that were never realized. What effect could this have on people and on your credibility?

Perhaps the greatest deterrent to using externally driven change is that you must commit to being the continuous, persistent driving force behind the change. You'll need to supply the motivating force for the entire process, until the change has become permanent. Anything less will result in an almost immediate return to the old way of doing things. This won't do much for your credibility, and it will create additional barriers to future change processes.

These negatives are only outweighed if the change is important enough, if you believe in it enough, and if you are willing to shoulder the burden of being the external driving force until others take up the banner, or until the results can speak for themselves.

Chapter 6
Political Barriers to Change

Some of the most trying problems to be faced in implementing change are political in nature. Included are all the difficulties related to special interests, whether arising from deeply held beliefs or some form of self-interest.

Those expected to make a change may hold personal beliefs that are at odds with the proposed change. Deeply entrenched patterns of thinking and behaving may have to shift radically if the change is to take hold. There may be career interests or subgroup identity issues involved. Whatever the source, however they manifest, political interests represent a major arena of practical barriers to the change process.

If a Change Cycle is to run its course, these political barriers need to be dealt with, one way or another. Here are a few suggestions based on my experience that may help. These ideas are not cure-alls, but they have worked in a variety of politically charged environments. Some of these ideas were discussed in the preceding chapter on imposed change, but they may take on greater significance viewed against the backdrop of a political setting.

First of all, it helps to assess the nature of the opposing political force. Is it a whole group or merely the leadership of the group that poses the barrier? Is the opposition to the change based on people's deeply held beliefs or is it motivated by self-interest? Once you have determined the nature of the opposition as best

you can, you have a much better chance of formulating a strategy
to deal with the barrier.

Political Opposition From Deeply Held Beliefs

If you're dealing with a deeply held belief that isn't likely to
change, your best chance for obtaining your objectives may lie in
some form of persuasion. This should be based on showing the
value of the change through demonstration. Can the opposition
be exposed to a situation where the change is in place and working
(e.g., a similar organization that has already implemented this
type of change)? Is it possible to demonstrate the effectiveness of
the change on a small scale—a simulation, prototype, or pilot
project—where the change can be observed and evaluated based
on live evidence? Demonstrations can take place early in the
change process, or they may be possible only when the change is
in place and its benefits can be observed in practice.

Of course, an opposing belief that is deeply felt may never
change, regardless of how effective the demonstration of potential
benefits may be. It would be equally difficult to convince
supporters of "right to life" or "freedom of choice" to shift their
respective positions based on any practical demonstration of the
benefits of the opposing position. When deeply held beliefs are
involved, actual shifts in position are rare, even though many
forms of accommodation may be possible.

When faced with sincere, belief-driven opposition to a desired
change, the options for dealing with it fall into these five areas:

◆ Try to shift the belief with compelling demonstrations of the
   value, potential, or benefits of the proposed change.
◆ Find some means of arbitration acceptable to both parties.
◆ Find a way to accommodate both positions simultaneously.
◆ Find a way to marry the differing points of view into a reso-
   lution or reconciliation that goes beyond any initial positions.
◆ Impose your will on the opposition.

Note that several of these means of dealing with deeply held
opposing viewpoints involve shifts from both parties.
Accommodation, creative resolutions, and third-party arbitration
all involve some shifting from your own initial position. If you

aren't willing or able to do this, or if you simply don't see the value in any modification of your original viewpoint, then you're left with rather limited options. You can convince others of your initial position, try to impose your will on them, or turn your attention to other matters that may prove more fruitful.

In most cases, it pays to hold the opposing point of view in high regard. Remember, we're still speaking of sincerely held positions based on deeply felt beliefs. By valuing the opposing force, you may stimulate your own creative process and that of the opposing parties. If you can identify a common purpose or a superordinate goal to which all parties align, it's quite possible to work together to find a mutually satisfying solution.

Resistance isn't necessarily a negative condition. In fact, the resistance of opposing forces is essential for creative solutions to problems to be developed. Without resistance in some form, a creative solution won't emerge, since there would be little to stimulate the creative process. (See Chapter 8 and Appendix, Part A, for a discussion of creativity.)

What about other options for achieving change when you're faced with opposition based on strongly held beliefs? As mentioned above, convincing others of the value of the change is most difficult when the opposition has strongly held beliefs. These beliefs may act as blinders toward whatever compelling evidence you present. Further, it may be that however good your demonstration of the potential or actual benefits of the change, holding on to the opposing belief may be more important to others than any benefits from the change. In short, trying to persuade people under these conditions has a relatively low probability of success.

When all else fails, your only remaining option may be to impose your will on the opposing parties. When strongly held beliefs are involved, this is particularly challenging. From the beginning to the end of the Change Cycle, an unrelenting effort is required to sustain movement. Since people will be making the change reluctantly at best, the effort to move them will require quite a bit of continuing pressure, monitoring of behavior, and likely negative consequences for non-cooperation.

Even if the Change Cycle can be completed at the level of behavioral change, such change is always subject to reversal if there isn't a corresponding shift in attitudes, beliefs, or values. As discussed previously, a government can suppress religious activity effectively for decades—even generations—but former practices will re-emerge once outside pressure disappears, so as long as the original beliefs and associated values remain intact.

When the beliefs and values involved are not so important, matters become far easier. In this case, there is a greater possibility of people agreeing to make a change, even if they don't believe in it. (A more thorough discussion of this point can be found in Chapter Five.)

Your best chance for moving forward with change despite deeply held opposing beliefs is through a process of creative resolution, accommodation, or outside arbitration. If you adopt a stance that the value of the change is greater than the value of holding to your starting position, the chances for successful implementation increase markedly.

Political Opposition From Self-Interest

Another basic condition of political opposition stems from self-interest, whether defined in terms of individual or group interests. In evaluating the nature of opposition to change driven by self-interest, a critical distinction needs to be made. Is this position based on reality or on ill-informed perception? This is not a philosophical point. In many instances all that is necessary to shift an opposing position is to share the same information that allowed you to arrive at your point of view.

Other times it may be necessary to go further by clearly communicating the value of the proposed change through elaborate vision statements or practical demonstrations of results and associated benefits. If the opposing point of view is based on misinformation or gaps in information, this sharing process and demonstration of value can be very effective.

There are, however, many instances in which no amount of information sharing or demonstrations of value are sufficient to change people's minds. There are several reasons why this may be true, but a common one is fear. Fear can literally blind people to the potential you've been trying to demonstrate. If fear is the motivation behind opposition, people may need several reassurances or demonstrations of protection from what they fear in order to let down their guard and begin to consider the change.

In the workplace, these fears often revolve around loss of one's job or interference with career objectives. In other cases, fear may be based on suspicion of the real motives behind the change. Just as you've been sizing up the nature of the opposition, they've been sizing you up. If your motives are in question, then all sorts of negative emotions, fear, and distrust are likely to spring up in opposition to whatever you propose, regardless of its merits.

If opposition to the proposed change doesn't respond to an influx of convincing information and demonstrations of value, you may have to look at your own credibility or your underlying motives to discover why people oppose the change. In truth, you may be unaware of all the factors that motivate you, and they may be getting in the way. Better to uncover these motives and deal with them yourself, than to let them continue to undermine your effectiveness.

Opposition Motivated by Petty Self-Interest

It's also possible that the opposition is motivated by petty forms of self-interest. We've saved this for last, because it's too easy to jump to this conclusion before exhausting other explanations and other means of dealing with the opposing force.

When petty self-interest is indicated, it's still advisable to do a little more examination before acting rashly. Is the person or group involved aware of their own motivation? Elaborate rationalizations are common, and can prevent people from understanding why they think and act as they do. Perhaps—just perhaps—it's worth one last shot at trying to work with a few blockers to arrive at some mutual understanding of the issue at hand and their viewpoint. People can and do learn and change as the result of interaction with others. If it doesn't work, then at least you know you've made your best effort.

Suppose you reach the point of believing your opposition is

purely and simply based on self-interest. Further, it isn't amenable to any of the methods suggested thus far. Also assume that you're as convinced as ever that the change you seek is vital, that it's worth going to special pains to secure. You may now be willing to consider all sorts of ways to exercise influence and force to overcome the opposition. Before acting, though, it may be worth your while to revisit the discussion of the pros and cons of imposed or externally driven change (see Chapter Five).

Barriers to your well-intentioned change efforts can be frustrating and costly. Understanding the nature of the barriers can help you choose the best strategy for overcoming them. In the next chapter, I'll discuss effective ways of achieving change by involving those who are most affected in the change effort.

Chapter 7

Developing Support for a Change Effort

In Chapter Five, we focused on externally driven change. As we've seen, change can be difficult to implement when the motivation or driving force is external to the people responsible for making the change. What is the alternative?

Let's look at change that is driven by the will of participants, as well as by the will of their leadership. The purpose of this chapter is to describe several techniques that are useful in gaining support for and commitment to a desired change effort. These methods are effective under a wide variety of conditions. I'll also discuss specific means for increasing commitment among willing participants during implementation, as well as among those who initially oppose the change.

Methods to Gain Initial Support for a Change Effort

Enthusiastic Sponsors Are Effective Change Agents

When people first become involved with a change process, they need to go through their own evaluation of its value, assessing its potential and figuring out how it will fit into their lives. If someone else has already gone through this assessment process and can give a compelling explanation of why he or she sees value in the change, it can facilitate the process for others. A persuasive sponsor's enthusiasm and strong belief can be highly contagious. If a similar change has been effective elsewhere, exposing people to the successful situation can be very convincing and can answer potential questions about implementation and benefits.

Vision Statements Provide a Holistic View of the Proposed Change

Another technique that can often help is the use of vision statements that describe the fully implemented change. People want to understand what it will be like to work under the new conditions, and want to measure their progress against some sort of standard. A brief, carefully worded statement of the desired end state can be used as a starting point. It sets the stage for a more detailed explanation of the completed change and expected benefits. This could be followed by group discussion and perhaps some reflection on the impact of this change on their jobs and the workplace in general.

You might need to use a comprehensive description of a vision. Operating principles or other types of directional guidelines for behavior may be worth developing if the change in question has far-reaching implications for task performance. Some examples of operating principles:

- Each business unit must stand or fall based on its own profitability.
- We will keep the new products pipeline full in order to ensure our future.
- We will become the technological leader in our industry.

It might also make sense to use stories to illustrate what it will be like in the workplace once the Change Cycle is complete.

But with all these various ways to work with a vision, the intent is the same: to provide a holistic view of the desired future state. A vision does not need to be in any particular format to accomplish this purpose, but it does need to provide people with a more complete picture of what you are trying to accomplish than is possible with a set of goals or a simple mission statement.

Major Change Requires a Formal Translation Process From the Vision to Each Person's Job

A more formal process designed to help people understand

what the vision will mean for their own jobs can be essential in setting the stage for a major change effort. This translation process is especially important if the change applies to many different types of jobs or work units. If the vision statement, explanations, or stories about the future are generic, people will still need to translate the vision into the specifics about their particular job. What priorities, functional responsibilities, action patterns, and relationships are expected to shift as part of this change process? What will my job be like when the changes are in place? What are the potential benefits of this change for me?

Through a guided process of translating the vision into specific detail for each work unit and each job, people can truly come to grips with the potential, benefits, and other practical implications of the proposed change. This process goes far beyond the usual orientation session, and can help build broader commitment. Once people understand the end state they are trying to create and how it affects them personally, they will find it far easier to develop plans to accomplish it. The holistic nature of vision statements and stories provides a more complete information base for understanding just what the change will look and feel like, and what the results will be.

Notice that this same set of initial commitment-building ideas applies equally well to people who have misgivings about the proposed change and those who do not. No one can be expected to commit wholeheartedly to a change without going through an initial evaluation of its promise and impact on his or her own life. Even if an initial degree of commitment is gained, it may wane unless nurtured, and may have to be guided and bolstered over time as the change process encounters practical barriers.

Continuing Methods to Persuade Others to Join Your Change Effort

Assume now that you have gone past the initial attempt to gain commitment both from participants and other interested parties who may have been opposed to the change. You cannot expect that everyone will be a committed supporter of the change. There will likely be those who still have their doubts, as well as opponents of the change who remain utterly unconvinced. Given this state of affairs, what can be done?

Let's consider first those people who are expected to participate directly in the implementation process. A continuing support system is essential throughout the implementation of the change. This may consist of corporate sponsorship, real time consulting assistance, backup resources, or any number of other means of practical support.

Upper-management sponsorship can be important in dealing with political barriers that develop as the Change Cycle proceeds. There may be need for special resource allocations or more time for completion of a given phase of the change process. High-level sponsors may need to visit occasionally to provide encouragement, as well as to find out firsthand what is going on.

Using Third-Party Support

Third-party support can take many forms and be valuable at all stages of the Change Cycle: identifying problems, dealing with practical barriers, acting as an objective observer during implementation, assisting with problem-solving efforts, and helping leaders keep the change process on track and moving. Even without extensive full-service consulting, facilitation can fill some often overlooked needs. There is certainly the need for facilitation of the translation process, and this includes continuing work with those who are unconvinced about the value of the effort. But there is also the need for frequent work-group discussions of problems and other issues that develop over time. Some of these discussions will go on while people are actually doing on-line tasks. But some discussions of implementation, group dynamics, and personal adjustment issues should occur in a setting better suited to reflection than the busy workplace.

It can be beneficial for a facilitator to be present at these off-line discussions. The facilitator, usually from outside of the group, can provide objectivity, push for clarity and resolution, and keep the group on task. Facilitated discussions are useful for the purpose of reviewing what has happened and for extracting what has worked, what has not worked, and why.

It may be appropriate to handle many knotty operational problems in this way, but a wide variety of other issues may be equally important to discuss in a dedicated setting. If the change process is to move forward swiftly and surely, it is important to capture these learnings, determine their implications, and apply them as continuous improvements to the change process. The more direct the linkage is between learning and application in the workplace, the better.

This dynamic sequence from events to outcomes, to evaluation, to learning, to feedback, and finally to adjustment, is at the heart of effective change management. The sequence needs to be on people's minds as they go through their daily work. Focused group processing helps develop the ideas and take full practical advantage of them. Everyone needs to recognize the importance of this sequence and to take responsibility for doing it. Facilitation of this sequence can be handled effectively in many ways, whether processing is led by a trained group leader or facilitator. It is quite feasible to fill all of these facilitation needs using well-equipped internal resources. What is important is that this function be performed well, not who does it.

Building Commitment Through Problem Solving and Feedback of Progress

Remember, the question we are dealing with here is commitment, not the broader issue of managing the overall change process. What do all of these discussions of problems, results, learning, and process improvement have to do with building and sustaining commitment? People respond to tangible proof. Every time something is learned and that learning is applied to what they are doing, there is a sense of real progress. Even though the Change Cycle hasn't yet run its course, and even though the next milestone of progress may not be in sight, there is tangibility here.

There is also a continuing need to deal directly and as quickly as possible with problems as they come up. The very act of bringing problems out into the open and exercising all of one's capability toward solving them builds commitment. When solutions are found and forward momentum is felt, it builds our personal commitment toward the whole endeavor. There is a continuous need in people who are engaged in a change process for these tangible signs of movement toward their desired goals. The ongoing processing of events for the purpose of moving the effort forward is a great means to build commitment and sustain momentum.

Celebrating Progress and Milestones

This same notion of finding tangible signs of progress can be applied in other ways as well. Milestones, intermediate goals and objectives, celebrations for moving past important barriers or from one stage of the Change Cycle to another are all appropriate ways to give people an ongoing sense of their progress. Some of the uncertainty of the journey into new territory can be addressed by keeping careful tabs on progress, feeding back any significant signs of forward movement, and celebrating real progress. These actions can effectively build team spirit among participants, result in greater satisfaction with the process of change, boost the level of commitment, and build momentum toward goals.

Real progress can be just the tangible proof naysayers need to begin shifting their attitudes toward the change. It can also serve as a visible demonstration of management's commitment and willingness to see the change through to completion.

Involving the Opposition

So far, we've focused on gaining commitment from the actual participants in the change process. What can be done to gain commitment, or at least agreement, from those who are still opposed but not directly involved in implementing the change? The key words here are *exposure, involvement,* and *translation.*

Special pains need to be taken to keep these people informed about what is happening in the implementation effort, beyond the usual progress reports or monthly summaries. What is needed is more direct exposure to the change effort itself, such as site visits or informal question-and-answer sessions with the project team. Involvement can go still further, including participation in team problem-solving sessions, or actually doing tasks in the new way.

The point here is that all this exposure and involvement helps address any information gaps or misperceptions that people may have. It also allows them to develop their own sense of ownership. For example, if someone comes up with just the idea that is needed to move the project past a critical hurdle, that person will probably feel a sense of personal pride and contribution as the project moves forward.

But there is still more that is needed in many cases. It helps a great deal if people can bridge the gap between their own situation and one that they are observing. If those who oppose the change are able to translate what is going on in a pilot project, let us say, to their own personal situation, many of their concerns could evaporate. Think what might happen if people could identify some concrete way that the pilot project could benefit them.

Example: Involvement With a Pilot Project Relieves Fears

Suppose a computer manufacturer was engaged in a pilot project to test the value of customer service hotlines. This project had been undertaken despite the continuing doubts and misgivings of a group of sales and service representatives. These people feared that an important responsibility of their own might be usurped by such hotlines, eroding their role as the primary source for after-sales customer support.

Imagine that one of these salespeople became involved with the pilot project enough so that she could begin to see how a hotline might help one of her customers. She might recognize that the hotline would be used primarily to solve just the kind of day-to-day, niggling problems that she abhors. She might begin to view the hotline as an adjunct to her job, one that could free her from having to deal with small issues that eat up so much time. She then could spend more time on client development or account penetration. By concentrating on major clients, helping to develop their plans for future large-scale computer systems, increased sales as well as an enhanced relationship with major customers could result. Perhaps she could shift attention toward dealing mainly with key decision makers rather than being spread thin dealing with small, daily operational issues.

Show Opponents How the Proposed Change Will Help Them

If people who initially oppose a change can see its value in accomplishing something of importance to them, then their position can shift markedly. The chances of this occurring are enhanced if this is literally an objective of those who are directly involved in implementing the change. It helps if this objective is explicitly stated, and the person(s) doubting the change can be involved in the process that pinpoints how the change can help them.

It is not hard to see how this process helps to clear the way for wider acceptance. Not only can the political barriers be lessened, but practical usage ideas can emerge. People can begin to see how the new idea could fit into their work lives in ways that were not obvious at the outset. New benefits may emerge and, along with them, broader enthusiasm and support for the change.

The Value of a Humane Approach to Change

The preceding section is focused on means of shifting the viewpoint of those who initially oppose a change. The means suggested so far have all been "soft". I don't intend to imply that more forceful ways of imposing one's will on others cannot overcome opposition. I have, however, a definite bias toward these more humane means. Under most conditions, humane means are the only ones that will truly work. The exceptions to this general state of affairs are considered elsewhere. (See Chapter Five, "Imposed Change".)

For the moment, let us focus on the value of a more humane approach to managing change. I am concerned here with the application of humane means wherever possible—throughout any change process and, by implication, any time people work together toward the accomplishment of some purpose. Humane does not always mean "soft", and it certainly does not mean easy, less effective, or slow. Humane refers to the intention behind the act. Humane means that the value of other people is kept in mind when means are considered. Humane means that we manage our own actions, according to a sense of responsibility to others as human beings like ourselves.

What is the practical value of this approach to change management? The first point is that a humane approach engages people's will more or less voluntarily, while imposed change often opposes people's will. Since the best chance for lasting, significant change lies in people wanting the change, it is far better to enlist people's support than to demand it.

The importance of will and commitment is difficult to exaggerate. It plays a critical role in driving the change process at each and every point throughout the entire cycle. Will also is a necessary component in the creative process, and in any mental process involving a focused effort to overcome resistive forces. (See Appendix, Part A for a discussion of the role of will in creativity.) This goes beyond the scope of realizing change in the workplace, and into many other aspects of our lives. Wherever people need to focus their energies and capabilities toward the accomplishment of some end, will plays a vital role. If you can focus people's will on accomplishing organizational goals, including implementing change, your chances for success improve greatly. The best way to do this, under most conditions, is through processes that draw people in rather than force people to do what is required. There are definite and severe limitations to when and where externally imposed change can work.

There are other compelling practical reasons to work with people to create internally driven change. By treating people humanely, you create the conditions under which more may be accomplished in the future. By building commitment and internal will to accomplish one purpose, you create receptivity for pursuing other goals in the future. Not only this, exercising one's will and capability toward accomplishing something you believe in can be a heady experience. Having experienced it once, people will want to experience it again and again.

As people strive to accomplish a goal that is a challenge to their capability, there may be a stretch involved. People may have to reach beyond their own experience base to find solutions.

They may have to tap their own intuitive and creative talents, or go beyond what they felt they were capable of accomplishing. This can be both exhilarating and addictive in a healthy way. What better preparation for the challenges of the future than a group of people who are looking forward to the next challenge?

But this whole optimistic scenario depends upon people believing in what they are doing—committing of their own free will to the process of change or the accomplishment of an objective, and applying their own will and capability to any challenges they encounter. Under most circumstances, you can accomplish more and better prepare the ground for future challenges through humane methods than through the imposition of external force. This should be enough reason to apply humane methods wherever possible.

Chapter 8

Intuition and Creativity in the Change Process

Whenever you face resistance to change, you will need to call upon all your capability to move the process forward. Intuition is a key component of our capability, but one that can be elusive and unpredictable. In this chapter, I'll introduce some techniques that can help you access and use your intuition.

Intuition is a capability that we all possess, a part of our everyday lives. Neither mysterious nor unapproachable, intuition can be integrated with other forms of thinking, such as linear and analytic processes. Intuition may be so much a part of our typical patterns of thought as to go unrecognized or to be taken for granted in examining how we think about things. In any case, intuition is more natural and accessible than many people think.

Intuition is part of any human endeavor in which we make judgments or decisions, or speculate on possibilities and potential. Intuition is present whenever we reflect upon experience or arrive at encompassing concepts. It is the thought process that allows understanding of the world and ourselves, despite an incomplete base of experience or knowledge. Intuition is applicable and most likely present, whether we know it or not, in almost every aspect of our lives.

Many people view intuition as something that may interfere with, rather than enhance, their thought process. Some believe their intuition is somehow out of their control. Intuitive insights may be viewed with skepticism, because they're sometimes off the mark or impractical. The fact that the intuitive process may sometimes miss the mark is no more reason to reject it than to reject linear thought because it cannot always provide the desired answers. Consider being open to using whatever capabilities are available to accomplish what you desire, rather than being concerned about which has the higher batting average.

The reasons for rejecting intuition have less to do with undervaluing its utility than with the feeling that it can't be controlled. An analytical method can be designed and followed step by step to the end. It may or may not yield the desired results, but analytical methods are orderly, replicable, and predictable. Intuition isn't. It may not operate when you wish, and its path is no more predictable than its results. In a sense, one must give up the feeling of control in order for intuition to operate.

The need to release control is the real barrier preventing many people from consciously accessing their own intuition. They may fear that relinquishing control over their mental processes for even a moment might somehow be dangerous. In short, some people find it difficult to simply trust in their own intuitive process. The techniques presented here are designed to help overcome this barrier but, in the end, each person must be willing to trust the intuitive process and let it operate.

Intuition and Receptivity

Intuition can be a valuable tool both within and outside the Change Cycle. I believe we all have intuitive capability. This discussion explores simple, practical ways of gaining greater access to your own intuitive powers. In exploring these ideas, keep in mind that there is no one formula for becoming more intuitive. But a few straightforward ways of structuring issues seem to create a state of mind conducive to intuitive insight.

These hints are based on my own experience and years of discussion with others. This is first and foremost a description of methods that have worked. If for no other reason than this, it's worth trying these techniques and drawing your own conclusions.

Intuition depends upon receptivity. Intuitive insights seem to flow into the mind, rather than be created by the brain. People speak of ideas that pop into their heads or of being touched by the muse. They describe moments when they simply know the right thing to do, without logical thought or conscious analysis. This isn't to say that all ideas are received in this way, that no ideas are generated by the brain itself. But here we're speaking of another type of brain function: that of *receiver*. Ideas do sometimes seem to flow into our minds from elsewhere. It doesn't feel as though we've created these ideas, but rather that we are vessels that the ideas enter. Ideas are then processed by the brain and are given expression.

Intuition is a tool, one that can complement your analytic abilities. You possess many different mental capabilities, and can train yourself to access the ones you need, when you need them. At times, the brain's analytic abilities are right for segmenting issues, examining each piece, and recognizing connections and patterns among the segments. In this way, you can organize quite a wonderful base for analyzing most issues. But purely analytic thinking falls short in providing a coherent picture of the whole.

Addressed analytically—whether a particular aspect of a situation is missing or undervalued, or the linkage among segments isn't fully understood, or the overall meaning and implications are unclear—something almost always seems incomplete. If you depend exclusively on analytic methods of understanding, a quality of completeness or evaluative meaning often will seem to elude you. By supplementing your analytical abilities with your intuitive abilities, you can fill in these gaps.

Defining the Problem to Stimulate Intuition

How can we access this intuitive process at will, as often as we desire? We may never be able to use as much of this potential as we'd like, but we can improve our effectiveness. One way is to crystallize the issue at hand. Think of this as isolating the issue and defining it as precisely as possible. Sometimes it helps to think of the issue in terms of two opposing forces:

Activating Force →← *Restraining Force*

The left arrow represents the driving or activating force, what you want to have happen. The right arrow represents the re-straining force, the resistance of barriers to be overcome. Clearly defining these two forces and holding them simultaneously in mind stimulates the intuitive process. The tension created by your desire pushing against a resistive force can arouse all of your capability, including your intuitive powers to resolve the issue. By holding this tension in mind, you're focusing your own will and simultaneously activating your own capability to overcome the barrier. An idea may come to mind, bringing the answer you seek.

Intuition in a Contract Negotiation: An Example

A few years ago, I was involved in lengthy labor contract negotiations as director of corporate development for a large transportation company. Several months were devoted to planning, several more months to carrying out an elaborate communication plan with the workers, and then more spent in actual negotiations. The effort had been rocky from the outset; even so, no one had foreseen just how difficult it would be to reach resolution. After struggling for nearly a year, management and labor remained at odds on the central issue: wages. With everything else substantially settled, the deadlock on the company's proposed wage cut had brought negotiations to a virtual standstill.

These negotiations took place just after deregulation of the transportation industry. The industry was undergoing a rapid and very depressing weeding-out process; companies large and small had failed. Surviving companies were confronting the fact that pre-regulation profit margins were a thing of the past. Rates were spiraling downward, with no end in sight to the downward trend line. Some companies responded by lowering wages to maintain some small margin of profitability. But where wages were governed by a union contract, as was the case here, there was little flexibility. Several unionized companies had been among the first to fail; their rates had become uncompetitive due to higher union wages and benefits.

Our management was adamant that a reduction in wages of

fifteen to twenty percent was essential for the business to remain viable. The union leadership was just as committed to its position that wages needed to be frozen at current levels. After long and fruitless negotiation, we appeared deadlocked. The old contract had expired. In fact, we were nearing the end of a second three-month contract extension. This was truly the eleventh hour: if we couldn't reach agreement soon, the workers would strike. The founder of the company had already indicated that if there were a strike, he might very well just close the doors and go out of business. We were clearly under plenty of pressure to come up with a resolution, and to do it immediately.

Days of fruitless negotiation had passed. It was now after nine p.m. and we were less than three hours away from a strike, with no solution in sight. A previous strike several years before had been violent, resulting in property damage and mistrust. Since that time, we had worked to rebuild trust and respect for each other. We were all determined to avoid another bitter confrontation. At a quarter past nine, we were staring at each other in stony silence. Utterly out of ideas, we were looking squarely at the probability of a strike no one wanted.

Finally, one of the managers moved to the easel and began writing. He didn't have a solution, but he had been able for the first time to boil down the wage issue into two simple statements:

Management	*Union*
15% reduction in wages → ← *same annual income*	

This wasn't the solution, but rather a critical step in the right direction. He had clarified and effectively communicated the basic problem: the seemingly irreconcilable tension between the absolute needs of management and the absolute needs of the workers. The room remained silent as everyone focused on the words scrawled on the easel. Then it happened.

A union representative blurted, "I've got it. What we need is a gain-sharing program. We take lower wages on a weekly basis, but make up for it through cost savings. We could work out some sort of quarterly reconciliation payment based on the money we save the company. The more we can reduce the company's costs, the bigger the quarterly check."

Hardly a moment passed before one of the managers had taken up the idea: "I know just where to save the money. There's literally millions of dollars we can cut from fuel costs, and the workers really control most of it. All they have to do is drive a little slower."

Over the next hour, we roughed out a basic agreement containing an ongoing weekly wage reduction, combined with a gain-sharing plan built around cost savings. The details took months to work out, and they didn't come easily. But the pivotal intuitive insight arrived in the moment just described. The workers ended up with a higher income under the new contract, and the business not only survived, but profits increased.

Using Thought Experiments to Achieve Insights

Everyone knows how to daydream. Thought experiments are simply daydreams with a mission. The difference is that daydreaming is random in nature and occurrence, while a thought experiment is purposeful. Because a thought experiment has a specific goal in mind, course correction takes place almost automatically. Unlike daydreams or unstructured stream-of-consciousness thinking, with thought experiments you remain aware of your objective and make modifications in direction along the way.

This isn't to imply that a linear or logical train of thought operates during thought experiments, but merely that you can refocus when a path unfolding is not reaching the objective. The purposeful nature of thought experiments encourages useful insights more than stream-of-consciousness thought does. You can activate a thought experiment consciously, or it may occur spontaneously when you focus attention on an issue or problem (e.g., an upcoming confrontation, a challenging meeting or presentation, surprising new information).

Once engaged, you may experience letting go of most conscious control of the thought process. Except for occasional corrections, the thought experiment will follow its own course. You can simply sit back and observe, as a spectator. This dual perspective of participant and observer permits a certain degree of objectivity. It can be a powerful and persuasive experience, like watching a movie of yourself. Since a thought experiment is performed in the privacy of your mind, you may feel free to experiment with actions and ideas that are different from your usual ways of behaving.

This is a safe enterprise. You don't have to share any ideas or results with others unless and until you are satisfied. Because of this freedom, it is easy to slip into the role of observer, one who stands somewhat apart from the action taking place.

As you practice this technique, it becomes possible to undertake three roles. First, instead of simply being a passive observer, you can begin directing the action and events. You can vary the situation and your actions and observe the results. Second, as a participant or star of the thought experiment, you can experience the situation. The third role you play, either simultaneously or after the thought experiment is finished, is that of critic. You may find yourself judging that certain choices are not appropriate, or that a different action could produce better results. As director, you can immediately redirect the thought experiment's path. Or you may choose to follow one train of thought to its conclusion, evaluate it, then change key variables and replay the scene.

Important insights can occur. You may notice behavioral patterns in yourself that you would like to change, either to correct faults or to make the most of your strengths. You may become aware of recurring responses that are not effective under certain circumstances. In this way, thought experiments can provide a means of personal development, as well as a planning tool for yourself. You are able to perceive things in a new light and this can leave undeniable impressions.

One of the nice things about thought experiments is that they are pleasant as well as effective. People can use this technique without much training or effort, since we all seem to have this ability. You need only a little awareness of its value for problem solving, and a little discipline in starting the process and keeping it on track. The benefits are great, the effort slight.

Using Thought Experiments to Test and Improve Ideas

Filling in gaps is only one benefit of thought experiments. Imagine that you have an idea, but you aren't sure just how it could play out in reality. Before committing energy and resources to a live trial, try your idea in a thought experiment. You can visualize how your new idea will stand up to inevitable practical resistance. Consciously vary the scenario, giving greater or lesser emphasis to one dynamic factor or another. Mental simulation increases your opportunities to explore variations that would be difficult to duplicate through live testing. What thought experiments lack in substantive results, they repay in breadth and variety of testing possibilities. Thought experiments provide great value as preliminary feasibility tests.

An idea that survives your thought experiment testing will be much stronger and more likely to work when you bring it to life. Thought experiments allow you to improve your ideas prior to public exposure. It is certainly easier to make changes in thought than to make modifications to pilot programs. If an idea doesn't work one way, mentally modify it and try again. You conserve time, energy, and other resources, while maintaining enthusiasm for the change process.

Thought experiments provide a way of pulling together ideas when you aren't clear just how they mesh. For example, suppose you're working with a group to create and communicate a vision of your factory after some major changes are implemented. You understand the implications for certain hard-number business results, but you don't fully grasp the impact the changes will have on the look and feel of the building, or what it would be like to work in the new environment. Having a few others imagine life in the factory following the anticipated changes might result in a more complete picture. Not only can people visualize the future state, but they may also perceive dominant interactive patterns in the new setting. Visualization can evoke elusive factors that defy analysis, such as emotional tone within the changed environment.

This simple technique can pinpoint barriers to implementation, or project how the dynamic factors of an issue might play out. The basic driving and restraining forces may instantly crystallize once implementation unfolds in the thought experiment. With imagination, you have the potential for isolating where and how breakdowns are likely to occur, and for assessing the cumulative impact of anticipated changes. You'd have much more difficulty clarifying these factors using only analytical means.

Stages of Intuitive Thought

Intuitive insights often occur in reflective moments. People from all walks of life report that important insights may occur at any time, often when least expected. However, the process leading up to the moment of insight does seem to follow a relatively consistent pattern.

The first stage of this process can be called immersion. Immersion occurs during a period of time when a subject or problem takes on great importance. The problem may completely dominate your thoughts. You may feel motivated to study the history and background surrounding the issue, and to pursue intensive analysis of any available data. You might interact with others or go solo.

As this period closes, you'll have internalized information—a data base and some preliminary hunches and judgments. Most important, you may have isolated the specific issue, and defined it in terms of desired accomplishments and barriers to overcome. The entire immersion process may take only a moment, or months, or even years. It depends upon the nature of the issue, how much background and understanding of the subject area you need, and your unique methods of mental processing.

Recognize, however, that the work of immersion is to discover the core identity of the issue, and to describe it concisely. You may even grasp that point of tension between its activating and restraining forces described previously as part of the creative process. The issue might be defined in other ways, but you aren't done until you've arrived at that intensely felt tension between what is desired and what is blocking that desire. Then you move on to the next stage, the incubation period.

During incubation, ideas take form and grow. Incubation may

last for a short time or it may extend for a long period. Sometimes the issue must ripen for awhile before being brought to fruition. Other times, once the issue has been precisely formulated and the tension increased, intuitive insight may occur almost instantaneously. For major scientific or artistic breakthroughs, the incubation process could take years. In most cases, some development time is needed before the moment of insight.

A process for isolating the issue and precisely defining the point of conflict to stimulate intuition was described earlier in this chapter. This process works well in everyday situations where no great scientific or artistic breakthroughs are required to solve a problem. This straightforward technique is designed to move as rapidly as possible through the preliminary stages, to the point where insights may occur.

After this incubation period, there may come the moment of insight. There are no guarantees here, only a description of what has happened over and over again to others in many different fields of endeavor. Insights often occur when least expected. They cannot be forced, only coaxed. Insights, great or small, occur through a receptive process that cannot be pushed. You can do the groundwork but, in the end, you cannot make it happen, you can only let it happen.

Encourage the Intuitive Capabilities of Those Working With You

The process leading up to intuitive insight obviously depends upon individual capability. But nothing prevents us from using our collective capabilities to resolve problems creatively in a group. Many individuals focusing on the same issue is a powerful means of multiplying individual capability. If you are the group leader, how can you facilitate this?

Managers recognize that people have great diversity in cognitive style. Some thrive on solo processing of problems, activating their own intuitive process with little external interaction. Others rely on interaction to formulate understandings. Some learn best from experiencing a practical situation, then reflecting on it either by themselves or with others. For others, direct experience is less important. They're more reflective by nature, and may require only reliable information in order to understand a particular problem and suggest good solutions.

The point here is not to describe all the major differences in the ways people process information and come to an understanding about the world around them. But managers need to recognize that such fundamental differences exist and to account for them in any change effort, especially when designing a process where the intuitive powers of many people can be tapped. Intuitive insights are an integral part of the change process, a means of solving problems throughout the whole change cycle.

When you are planning a group process to bring intuitive thinking to bear on a common problem, consider how each member of the group processes information. Try to accommodate people who thrive on direct experience as well as those who operate well from written materials or an oral information base. Consider who works best alone and who needs the stimulation of interaction. Ask the participants what they need to be at their best. This will likely call for extra planning time and effort, but it is an investment that should pay off in productive group problem-solving processes.

Identifying the Process That Works Best for You

Personal effectiveness depends in large part on your ability to exercise your own talent. Understanding where and how you function best can be a major factor in leveraging your abilities, both analytic and intuitive. If you know what process works best for you, situations can be found or restructured to take full advantage of your strengths.

If you don't already know this, how can you find out? This can be a fascinating and rewarding exploration. First, scan your own experiences where you have tried to accomplish something difficult. Recall situations in which you accomplished what you set out to, and really enjoyed the process. How did you go about doing each one?

Do you recognize a recurring pattern across all of these success experiences? For example, you might find that in many cases you were able to work alone, without any time pressure, but with a clearly defined task and ready access to relevant information and resources. Or perhaps in each of your success experiences, you were a member of a closely knit team that met frequently and set its own agenda and priorities. Maybe you've joined existing teams as an expert in a subject area with which you are comfortable. Or perhaps you discover that the only times you have both felt good about the experience and accomplished what you set out to do, you've initiated, structured, and implemented the process largely on your own.

You may identify only a few common characteristics of these past success experiences, rather than some overarching pattern, but this can still be useful. Suppose you're only clear that you enjoy working with other people rather than alone, and that you function well as long as there is no intense deadline pressure. Even though this is an incomplete picture, it can help in choosing how you prefer to deal with issues.

You can use the thought experiment technique to discover your most effective process. Imagine yourself in an ideal setting. Are you active or reflective, alone or with others, in charge, or operating as part of a team? Is the task simple or complex, short-term or long-term? What is expected and required of you? What form of information are you using? Does the mood feel intense or low-key? Do you feel the exhilaration of being stretched to your limits or are you safely within your comfort zone?

These are just a few questions you might ask as you try to identify the key aspects and dominant patterns in the experience you're living in thought. You may have to run a few of these thought experiments before clear patterns emerge, but this isn't hard. You have much to gain and little to lose.

Other people can help you zero in on situational variables that help or hinder you in using your natural talents. This is especially true of people who know you well or have seen you operate in a variety of settings. They may be able to pinpoint factors that you've undervalued or ignored. Blind spots can only be pointed out by others; through this interaction, we fill in these gaps in our understanding.

Each of the three methods just mentioned—analyzing successful experiences, thought experiments, and asking others—use both intuitive and non-intuitive capabilities to help you understand yourself. A great deal can be learned by scanning our experiences, or those that we can imagine, and drawing logical, analytical conclusions. We can discover similarities, linkages, and simple patterns by analyzing these experiences. However, intuition allows us to go further. Overarching patterns or pointed insights are more likely to surface during intuitive rather than analytic processing. Aside from these insights, interpretations and judgments about your discoveries also depend upon intuitive capability rather than analysis.

Differences Between Intuition and Creativity

Throughout this book, I make references to both intuition and creativity. The distinction between the two should be clarified. Intuition refers to the process by which we access non-logical, non-analytical thought. The products of intuition include ideas that are new to us, judgments, holistic understandings, emotionally toned realizations, and other thoughts that aren't derived strictly from structured thought.

Creativity is the process by which we use all our capability to resolve problems, where a special effort is needed to overcome resistance. Any time we are blocked from attaining a desired objective, the creative process may be triggered. If our desire is strong enough and our capability sufficient to the task, we will find an answer or a resolution. The capability involved in the creative process may include, but is not limited to, intuition.

As with intuition, creativity appears to be part of our everyday lives. It isn't restricted to phenomenal insights, theories, inventions, or works of art. The creative process certainly results in products, but the products needn't be earthshaking in their implications or utility, nor do they need to be utterly new either to the world or to the person involved. Once the definition of creativity is expanded this way, we can easily see that creativity operates in all of our lives, and that it isn't at all rare. This doesn't detract from the value of extraordinary creations, but it does point to the fact that the ability to access the creative process is available to us all.

Intuition plays a role throughout the Change Cycle, and is intimately tied into the creative process. Intuition allows us to go beyond analysis, supplementing it with a more comprehensive understanding. Intuition isn't an accessory, but a fundamental tool. With intuition working for you, your tool kit for directing change is more versatile and more complete.

Final Thoughts

This book was written for people who are face-to-face with the difficult task of leading change. If this was a straightforward task or one that was easily mastered, you would not have read this book. If I did not believe the book could make a difference for you, I would not have written it. The notion of a predictable cycle of change with a known set of dynamics is compelling because it offers us a better way of managing and controlling change. We can exercise our talents within a known framework and increase our chances of accomplishing whatever we want.

But the power of these ideas as an integrated set is easier to grasp through experience than through reading. The benefits of the Change Cycle will only become clear after you have used this process to implement a change of your own. If you give these ideas a fair trial, I believe they will work for you, just as they have for my clients and associates.

Looking back on the book, I am struck by how much has not been expressed. There is more to say about how to apply these ideas to organizations, to the issues confronting the world, and to our own growth and development. There are other effective techniques for managing change processes, as well as for managing ourselves. There is a great deal yet to understand about how to get change efforts back on track when they falter. But despite all that has not been covered, there is plenty here for you to try out for yourself. For my part, I'll keep wrestling with these issues and keep writing. Finishing this book signifies both an ending and a beginning for me. I hope your completion of this book represents the beginning of a new cycle for you, as well.

Once we allow for the notion of ourselves as creative or potentially creative people, we can face the world with a different attitude toward what is possible, not only about what we are capable of individually, but about what we can accomplish together in the world. Once we accept that we're capable of creative solutions, we can leverage this capability in new ways. In a world filled with effective problem solvers who believe in themselves and in their abilities, there is no telling what we could accomplish.

APPENDIX

Theory Behind the Change Cycle

Part A
Change Cycle Theory

As you no doubt have recognized by now, the Change Cycle model can be used to understand and manage many kinds of change, as long as the change is directed by conscious desire. But why does this model work? Where did it come from? For those who would like to know more about the theoretical underpinnings of the Change Cycle, I've included this appendix. If you prefer not to read this section, be assured that Chapters One through Eight have given you all the practical information you need to apply Change Cycle techniques to change in your business, government agency, or other organization.

Eight fundamental energies are at play throughout the Change Cycle. These eight energies can be thought of as physical energies that permeate the world. Each energy can play many different roles, but each has its own recognizable characteristics. While these eight energies play essential roles in the Change Cycle, I believe they also are vital in many other processes found in nature. We will examine their basic characteristics, as well as their roles in two closely related processes: creativity and the Change Cycle. The chart below lists the energies and corresponding stages in the Change Cycle, and shows which energies are essential in the creative process.

Chart 4. Stages of the Change Cycle and the Eight Energies

Stages of the Change Cycle	Energy	Forces in the Creative Process
1. Choosing the Target	Allowance	✓
2. Setting Goals	Will	✓
3. Initiating Action	Capability	✓
4. Making Connections	Connectedness	
5. Rebalancing to Accommodate the Change	Harmony	
6. Consolidating the Learning	Evolution	
7. Moving to the Next Cycle	Transition	
	Chaos	✓

In the following discussion, sometimes I'll refer to these eight energies as forces. When the energies are involved in the Change Cycle, they play out as dynamic forces throughout the whole process. They also define the dominant state of being for each stage of the Change Cycle. Similarly, some of these energies are present as dynamic forces whenever the creative process is going on.

Each of the eight energies plays a vital role in the Change Cycle. We will begin by describing Allowance, Will, Capability, and Chaos, and how these four forces explain the conditions necessary for change to occur. Then we will examine how these same four energies are always involved in the creative process. Keep in mind as you read that an intimate relationship exists between the creative process and the Change Cycle. The creative process is the means by which the Change Cycle moves along. Each time you encounter a challenge to be met, a problem to be solved, a barrier to be overcome, the creative process comes into play as the means to resolve the issue and move on. Without the creative process, there would be no Change Cycle, for movement in the desired direction would halt whenever resistance was encountered.

Dynamic Forces of Creative Change

Allowance (Practical Terminology: Choosing a Target)

The first of the forces is one of hope—of expanding potential. It is the principle of new horizons, of untried and unproved insights, the energy that allows for the birth of a new idea. We may call this first dynamic force Allowance. The term Allowance also refers to the state of being in which new ideas and possibilities are allowed into the mind for consideration. This state is both exciting and full of flux and uncertainty.

Allowance is embodied in new thought, without judgment of its practicality or limitations. It is the energy encompassing and facilitating a new idea before it is completely formulated, and before it meets with opposition ("yes, but…"). In order to start something new, the quality of Allowance must be present. Without it, there can be no creativity, and no guided change process. To imagine a world without Allowance is to imagine a world without new thoughts, without movement, without guided change. There could be random or unguided change, but not movement in a desired direction toward a desired outcome.

Will (Practical Terminology: Setting Goals)

While Allowance is a necessary component in any change process, it is certainly not sufficient unto itself. It must first be guided or directed. The second dynamic force that provides this direction can be called Will. Will is the energy of clarified visions, goals, and as-yet-unrealized desires. It is the driving force of desire or motivation as it manifests in human beings.

The qualities of direction and impetus are contained in Will. Will is a static force, yet one that implies the potential for movement toward a desired objective or future state. Will can't exist until there is a formulated end and an identified direction toward that end. This doesn't imply there must be an identified means of achieving the desired end. It simply says that a drive or directional force is established toward a desired outcome.

Will provides direction and impetus to the recognized potential of Allowance. Will also provides definition and focus to the flux of Allowance. Without Will, there could be no guided, non-random change process and no creativity.

Capability (Practical Terminology: Initiating Action)

The third force needed for the creative process to take place is the power of individual or collective Capability. Just as the force of Will supplies the sustaining power and guidance to the force of expanding potential called Allowance, Will is itself supplemented by and dependent upon the power of individual or collective Capability. This refers to the instrumental capability of any individual or the collective capability of a group, as applied toward an end. In other words, the force of Will helps to define the desired outcome, while individual or collective Capability provides an essential component of the means to accomplish that objective. Will without Capability cannot actualize potential. Similarly, Capability without the focus and direction provided by Will is just as incomplete. These three forces or energies provide cornerstones for our understanding of creativity and the non-random change process. Together, as a balanced set, they help explain the driving forces and the primary means for achieving change. But the interaction of these three forces will not gel into a powerful, dynamic process unless a fourth force is present in sufficient quantity. This fourth force is called Chaos.

Chaos (Practical Terminology: Resistance)

In order to understand the dynamics of the creative process, as well as how the whole Change Cycle operates, we must understand the energy form of Chaos. Notice that when each of the other seven energies becomes dominant within the Change Cycle, it defines a stage of the process. Chaos is different, in that it plays a vital role throughout all stages, but as a counterbalancing force. Chaos serves this same function in the creative process, counterbalancing the forces of Allowance, Will, and Capability.

In a sense, Chaos stands apart from the other energies of the change process, since each step in this process is defined by the dominance of one of the seven other energies. For example, when Will becomes the dominant energy at the second stage of the Change Cycle, its characteristics are more pervasive and apparent than the other energies, even though these others are certainly present to some degree. But even though Chaos doesn't define any one stage of the Change Cycle, it is absolutely essential throughout the process. No process of nature stands apart from and is not influenced by Chaos, and there are even situations in which Chaos is dominant.

The energy of Chaos interacts continuously with the other energies. They couldn't exist if it were not for the presence of this counterbalancing force. One way to view Chaos is as the opposite pole of each of the other energies. That is, Chaos is anti-Allowance, anti-Will, and so forth. Chaos as an energy exists at all points in the universe and pervades all natural processes. It may or may not dominate. Within the Change Cycle, Chaos must continually be counterbalanced by other forces; otherwise it will tend to dominate and the change effort will fail.

Chaos acts as a continual potential barrier to any ongoing process. In order for any change process to move forward in a desired direction, it must push against Chaos. The process must have enough driving force of its own to overcome the resistance created by the presence of Chaos. In order to move in any desired direction, in order to create new forms, Chaos must be overcome. Chaos plays a vital role at each stage of the Change Cycle. One way to think about Chaos is in relationship to each of the other seven energies. Chaos acts in opposition to the dominant energy of each stage. Chart 5 summarizes these relationships.

Creativity as a Means of Overcoming Chaos

I would like to describe how the creative process works as an interaction of the energies of Allowance, Will, Capability, and Chaos. Creativity as used here refers to the entire process of gaining understanding and insight to overcome the force of Chaos. There is a broad arena in which this definition of creativity can be usefully applied.

First, the creative process takes place throughout the Change Cycle, appearing at each and every point where people are face-to-face with resistance to their desired outcomes. In this way, creativity may be thought of as a primary means of engaging with opposition encountered along the path to change. It is the means by which the basic conflicts of each stage are overcome.

Aside from the way creativity plays out in the Change Cycle, it is important to expand the conventional usage of the term "creativity." An idea, action, or product needn't be new to be called creative. It need only address the resistive force of Chaos effectively. The idea or implied action itself may be one that has been used many times before, without limiting its effectiveness in dealing with the immediate need.

Creativity can take place with or without the conscious knowledge of the people involved. In other words, whether people are aware of it or not, the creative process is occurring on a daily basis in their lives. Any time someone must come up with a solution to overcome the resistive forces blocking the attainment of their desires, creativity is operating. It may not be anything more than dealing with daily annoyances, such as a car that won't start. It may, on the other hand, be used in a highly conscious way to deal with major scientific, artistic, or technological questions or issues in one's life.

Chart 5. Chaos in Relationship to the Other Seven Energies During the Change Cycle

	Dominant Energy	Traits of Chaos
Stage 1.	Allowance	Tends toward status quo. Unreceptiveness to new possibilities.
Stage 2.	Will	Dispersive force. Defocusing impact.
Stage 3.	Capability	Thwarts exercise of personal and collective capability. Disempowering force.
Stage 4.	Connectedness	Tends toward isolation. Blocks linkages, obscures connections.
Stage 5.	Harmony	Agitating and destabilizing force. Tends toward imbalance and disharmony.
Stage 6.	Evolution	Tends to push backwards toward older forms. Tends to block recognition of new emerging form.
Stage 7.	Transition	Tends toward holding pattern. Blocks recognition of the potential of the next cycle.

Creativity is an important ally operating in all aspects of human endeavor. It enables us to use all of our capability toward accomplishing an objective. As discussed in the previous chapter, part of this capability is commonly called intuition. The role of intuition in the creative process is one that can scarcely be exaggerated. Allowance depends to a large extent upon intuition as the means of bringing in new ideas and selecting among them. Intuition isn't the only source, but it is a major one. Will depends upon intuition to help make judgments, define goals, and focus desire. Intuition is a key capability that enables us to supplement linear and logical thinking when pushing toward resolution.

Intuitive ideas and judgments would mean little to us without Allowance. On the other hand, Allowance would be a largely empty state of being without the new ideas provided by the intuitive process, as well as by other sources. Intuition is, therefore, a major component of one's capability. Since the creative process plays out at every point in the Change Cycle, and since intuition plays a major part in Allowance, Will, and Capability, it would not only be difficult to exaggerate its importance, it would be impossible to eliminate intuition from the change process. (see Chapter Eight).

This broader definition of creativity also means that it is a natural part of our lives. Everyone has access to this creative process, and uses it frequently. Obviously, some ideas, actions, and products that result from this process are rare or more important to the world than others. But that doesn't negate the fact that the same fundamental process is accessible and used by all of us.

In all cases, the qualities of Allowance, Will, and Capability can be seen operating to overcome whatever resistance stands between us and what we desire. Think of each of these energies as supplying a necessary component of the creative process. We may recognize an idea that is better than what already exists. If so, a gap is created between the new and better concept and the current state of what exists. This gap represents potential; the larger the gap, the greater the potential. On a human level of perception, we recognize the possibility of something better than the current state, and we want to bring it into reality.

Dynamics of the Creative Process

Let's focus for a moment on the dynamics of the creative process as it might play out for a person trying to create something new. Imagine that we could slow down this process and observe it as a sequence of interactions among the forces of Allowance, Will, Capability, and Chaos.

First, Allowance would come into play. A new idea would be allowed to enter the mind for consideration. As soon as the new idea's potential has been recognized, the force of Chaos comes into play. In this case, objections to the new idea spring to mind. Limitations of all sorts surface in opposition to the new thought. If the idea has anything to do with bringing something new into the world, the objections are likely to be practical in nature. Implementation problems of all sorts raise doubts as to the feasibility of the idea, regardless of how much potential it might have in the abstract. It is impossible to bring anything new into existence without overcoming the resistive force of Chaos. And so a dynamic tension is now in place: the emerging desire for something new and better must push against the practical barriers to realization.

Once a dynamic tension exists between Allowance and Chaos, the other two major forces must come into play in order to resolve the tension. Only by exercising Will and Capability can Chaos be overcome and the creative process be complete. Said another way, the way to overcome practical barriers to the new idea is to exercise one's Will and Capability. The first step is to focus and amplify Will by clarifying what you wish to create. This often takes the practical form of setting specific goals that seem attainable, articulating why those goals are worthwhile, and describing how they can be achieved.

After the force of Will has been focused and amplified, Capability is the instrumental means—the "how to"—of overcoming Chaos, while Will represents the motivational means. If Will supplies the impetus and direction for the effort, Capability supplies the muscle power.

The dynamics of the creative process are diagrammed in the following chart. The opposing arrows represent the forces of

Allowance and Chaos, while the vertical arrow represents Capability playing the role of the instrumental means of resolving the conflict between Allowance (the activating desire for the change) and Chaos (the resistance to that change). Will is depicted as the force which holds the process together, focusing one's attention and capability on the clearly defined issue.

The Value of Chaos

Chaos thus acts as a check on the creative process and all directed change processes. This force acts to assure that there is significant driving force behind any change in form or structure. If Chaos weren't present, it would certainly be easier to produce new ideas or new forms, but there would be less energy behind many of these new ideas. As a result, there would be less value, less utility, and less importance attached to each of these new forms or ideas. Each step taken in a desired direction would mean less, and therefore would be less easily recognized or used.

Why is this an important point to bring out? Simply because the change process itself is so important. The changing of concepts, perspectives, and forms represents the fundamental way the universe moves, develops, and transforms itself. This resistive force of Chaos, acting as a check on the change process, assures that the changes that do occur are highly valued and represent a significant act of will.

Without Chaos, the act of creation, the product itself, and the directional movement implied by each change in perspective, ideation, or form would become trivial. The weight of value would shift from growth, development, self-discovery, and creativity to mere existence within a continually shifting set of circumstances. Individual forms would indeed shift, but little importance would be attached to such shifts. Self-discovery would occur, but without the emotional rush signifying its great importance to the individual having the insight.

With this in mind, it is possible to view the energy of Chaos as one that gives meaning and value to life. It is the energy that makes life, growth, and self-discovery take on great importance within all aspects of existence in general, and within our individual

Chart 6. Dynamics of the Creative Process

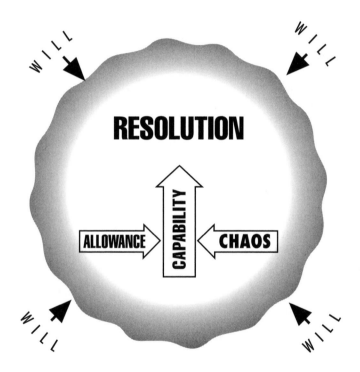

life experiences in particular. Far from being a force merely representing disorder, randomness, decay, and resistance, Chaos must also be viewed as the force that gives value to each of the other forces we have introduced, as well as to the whole process of change, and the new concepts and forms that result from this process.

Let's return now to the four remaining fundamental energies that comprise the rest of the Change Cycle: Connectedness, Harmony, Evolution, and Transition. The contribution of each of these energies to the Change Cycle will be discussed, and the interaction of Chaos with each will be examined.

Connectedness (Practical Terminology: Making Connections)

The energy of Connectedness provides the linkages among everything in the universe, resulting in a continual state of interaction. The term "interaction" refers to the state of being that is created because of the existence of this energy. Both terms (the state of being of interactivity and the energy or force of Connectedness) are used to describe this phenomenon.

This idea is similar to the notion of interconnectedness as it is used to describe natural ecosystems. Everything within an ecosystem is intimately linked. A change in any part of the system affects, to some degree, everything else in that system. Connectedness can be thought of as cosmic glue, or the binding force between all objects. Considered as a natural force, Connectedness always has the physical property of attraction.

This invisible bond makes it possible for anything influencing one part of the world to affect all other parts to at least some extent. The existence of this energy also implies that when one part or aspect of existence shifts—whether the shift is permanent or not—that shift has some degree of impact on all else. Since Connectedness is always present, the state of interaction is always present to some degree. Without this energy, patterns of change could exist independently at various points in the world. Patterns of change would find their absolute boundaries within a particular individual, circumscribed series of events, field of endeavor, or biological or physical process. If such boundaries did exist, the spread of change would be far more difficult to achieve.

The existence of this energy implies that all such boundaries are arbitrary. One can set such boundaries as a means of simplifying the understanding of a specific aspect of existence but, in truth, the ripple effect of any change in any one aspect of the world has some ultimately understandable and measurable effect on every other aspect. We study one aspect or another only to simplify the task of understanding reality, not because any particular aspect of our world can be completely understood through such delimited study. One such example, mentioned above, is a biological ecosystem. There is an interdependence among all aspects of an ecosystem, and a change in one aspect affects the others.

And so the condition of interaction opens the door to explore the interrelatedness of all that exists. It opens the door to explore how changes in one field of human endeavor profoundly—or only tangentially—influence other fields of endeavor. Similarly, since all aspects of existence are bound together, it implies at least some degree of commonality in the response to a given change across all aspects of existence.

Let's assume there is some degree of physical connection between all aspects of the universe we live in. Some of these connections are slight, while others are of profound significance. The point here is that an actual connection likely does exist, and therefore implies some impact on the whole, whenever change takes place in any part of the whole. Accepting this principle is analogous to accepting the Freudian notion of causality—that, for example, any slip of the tongue should be examined not as a random chance occurrence, but as though there is an identifiable cause for that slip of the tongue. You can make many discoveries about why people behave as they do once you assume there is cause behind such events, rather than accident or randomness. You needn't believe that such causality always exists. It is simply an assumption that is useful in stimulating thought and discovery.

In a similar way, once you begin looking for connections between significant changes or trends across the various aspects of our world or between fields of human endeavor, the door opens to profound discoveries. It is not necessary to understand all the connections at all levels of existence, to gain great value from this point of view. The value lies in gaining and using insights that might otherwise remain unexplored. All that is needed is a mindset or readiness to explore the possibility of such relatedness between two or more parts of our world.

It is interesting to look at Chaos in relation to Connectedness. While Connectedness binds things together, Chaos tends to block linkages, obscure connections, and isolate things. While Connectedness has the dynamic property of attraction, Chaos has the property of repulsion.

Harmony (Practical Terminology: Rebalancing to Accommodate the Change)

The fifth energy in the sequence of the Change Cycle is called Harmony. This term refers to the state that exists when all the key elements in a defined system are in balance with one another. Let's start with how Harmony relates to the other energies of the Change Cycle. It is particularly important to look at the role of Harmony in the functioning of relatively independent systems. (The terms "defined system" and "relatively independent system" are used to indicate that systems do interact with one another, and therefore aren't entirely closed.) While the fourth energy in the sequence of the Change Cycle, Connectedness, signifies the linkages among all elements of a system, the fifth, Harmony, signifies the notion of balanced interaction and relationships between the elements. One must have the linkage between elements in a system before one can concern oneself with the balance in the relationship between these elements.

Balance is a key to evaluating and shifting the dominance patterns of forces within a defined system. It also applies to the balance or Harmony that exists between systems—for no system exists in an utterly independent state. Since all systems are somehow connected (as implied by the fourth energy, Connectedness), there is always a relationship between systems that can be described in terms of degree of balance, harmony, mutuality, and so forth. Hence, wherever more than one identifiable system exists, there is a relationship that also exists and can be defined partially in terms of degree of harmony/disharmony. The only difference in looking within a given system versus looking across systems is in the scale of the factors that are being balanced—not the existence of these factors.

Now, just as there is an actual differentiated energy form for each of the previous forces, Harmony also exists as an energy form. This energy exists as a balancing force in nature with or without any intervention, recognition, or analysis by us. We can, however, optimize the impact of this energy through our awareness of its presence and judicious manipulation of events to take advantage of its presence.

If we examine our world as it exists today, we might question the existence of Harmony. That is, the magnitude of this energy's impact on our lives seems to be quite out of balance. Considered as a force, Harmony seems to be overwhelmed by other forces, and appears to be recessive in the overall scheme of things in our world. It is often hard to notice Harmony in a world filled with crime, illness, poverty, war, and massive inequity. Nevertheless, Harmony does exist and can be better used by us to move events toward our desired outcomes. Once the nature of all these energies and how they relate to each other is understood, it may be possible to bring the force of Harmony toward an optimum balance to help create more powerful and sustainable resolution of the issues facing us.

Harmony is essentially characterized as peaceful, contemplative, and stable. Other energies such as Allowance and Capability are far more dynamic in nature, compared to Harmony. When Harmony dominates a situation or a state of being, that situation will tend to be relatively stable. It will tend to maintain its current state of balance or resolution, unless destabilized by other forces. Thus, you may think of Harmony as an energy that tends toward increasing inertia. It will not shift of its own accord, but must be influenced by other factors before a change occurs. A system thus stabilized by the prominence of Harmony will tend to endure until it is acted upon by other forces. The role of Chaos in relation to Harmony is to act as an agitating and destabilizing force.

Evolution (Practical Terminology:
Consolidating the Learning)

The sixth energy can be described using the notion of Evolution. The concept of Evolution as it is used here depends upon an understanding of stability and mutability as they play out in the world. Any form or structure—an idea, a system, a material or energy construct—will be able to hold its recognizable existence for a period of time, but will also be subject to continual change. New forms can come into existence, and will inevitably be followed by even newer forms. But any form of existence will also maintain a relative stability—it will be recognizably the same—for a time, until the continuous transformation process of evolution gradually acts upon it to create new forms.

Thus, Evolution is an energy that is continuously present, whether we are aware of change taking place or not. As a dynamic force, it has both active and stabilizing properties, stabilizing in the sense that any form will seem to be the same for a time, even while it is changing to a new form. When the energy of Evolution is dominant, an identifiable form will not regress to an older form, but will maintain its identity over a span of time. It will, in essence, resist the forces of regressive change acting upon it. On the other hand, the energy of Evolution also is the active and relentless force behind the continuous change process in nature. This energy continually inundates all that it touches with newness.

Evolution is thus the energy of transformation—not the transformed energy or substance, but the force that lies behind the transformation process. Without this energy, there would be no sustainable change process. New ideas, new systems in nature, would slip back to older, established forms, or drift aimlessly from one form to another. The role of Chaos in relation to Evolution is to push backwards, to obscure the significance of change that has been accomplished, as well as any emerging form.

When the Change Cycle is described using practical terminology, the sixth stage is called "Consolidating the Learning." This refers to the process of understanding the change that has just occurred (the newly stabilized form and the process that led to the change), and what changes could come next (possible future forms and ways of creating those changes). At this stage of the Change Cycle, the change is already manifest, and people can more easily recognize and understand the change that has taken place. At the same time, it is easier at this point of the Change Cycle to look forward to what new changes might be built upon what has already happened. In this way, the currently stable forms created as the result of the change cycle are grasped more fully, and the possibilities of future changes begin to be understood.

Transition (Practical Terminology: Moving to the Next Cycle)

The seventh of these energies can be thought of as Transition. Transition is the energy that helps bring all the other forces into a wholeness and a final form, before moving on to another form or another cycle of change. The energy of Transition has a fleeting quality to it—as though by asserting itself, it causes its own dissipation or demise. This means that Transition (as a stage in the Change Cycle or as a dominant state of being) exists only as a passing state, for as one idea, structure, or form is finalized, it is simultaneously being prepared for what is to come next.

Thus, this energy of Transition is by its nature elusive. When it is dominant in a process, it is only a momentary phenomenon. When it is present at other times during the change process, it is difficult to detect in any way. It only exists in its full essence at the moment when an idea, form, or relationship has found its natural point of wholeness and completion.

The energy of Transition acts to draw together that idea, form, or relationship into its purest, most complete statement. This force serves to essentialize all the other forces into fully realized forms. It thus represents and helps bring about the culmination of the change process. It works in concert with the other energies to provide the actual completion of any cycle of change, as well as the feeling of completion to participants in any change process. It acts to help focus and essentialize what has come before while setting the stage for the next cycle.

Think of Transition as following Evolution in a sequential pattern, but also preceding the energy of Allowance. The last stage of the cycle, Transition, pulls together all that has gone before, and creates the conditions needed for the emergence of Allowance. This emergence of Allowance to a dominant position signifies the beginning of the next cycle of change. We can view the energy of Transition as the bridge between one cycle of change and the next.

This energy is unique in that it has many seemingly paradoxical qualities existing simultaneously. Transition is both passive and active, the end and the beginning, a culmination and a point of departure. It both sums up the old and presages the new. Transition can't exist without the presence of the other forces, but it has the ability to act on and transform all that has come before. Its presence makes the difference between merely having all the pieces of the puzzle in your possession or seeing them joined to create a picture as a unified gestalt. It signifies and makes possible the difference between knowledge and wisdom.

The effect of Chaos in relationship to Transition is to keep the process on the cusp between the two cycles—to block movement to the next cycle.

Part B

Structure, Dynamics, and Context of the Change Cycle

In the preceding section, the eight energies were introduced and the creative process was described. Throughout the book there have been points made about how these energies interact and relate to one another, and how they manifest in the world around us. But these ideas have been integrated with other subject matter. This section pulls those pieces together so that they can be explained more fully and examined on their own. In addition, other implications of the Change Cycle are explored. What does the Change Cycle imply for understanding stability versus change, states of being, and the impact of Chaos?

Random Versus Non-Random Change

The eight energies introduced in Part A of the Appendix interact within any process that produces change. The Change Cycle describes change that is non-random, resulting from conscious will. But there is other change that can occur outside the Change Cycle paradigm—change that is random, lacking a defined pattern or direction. This random change occurs independently of individual or collective desire. The important distinction isn't between change in the physical world and change in the realm of ideas. Rather, the distinction is between change that occurs as a result of choice or decision as opposed to change that is caused by the ongoing interaction of physical laws acting upon a set of existing conditions.

The eight energies and the laws describing how they interact with each other and the substance of the universe (whether the substance is an energy or material form) will continuously produce movement, representing both directional change and random change. Random change results in both the creation of new forms and possibilities, as well as the ending of older ones. However, random changes rarely build upon each other to form linked cycles of change, the way directed change does.

Sequence

The forces of change are presented here in a purposeful sequence that underpins any developmental or change process. Beginning with Allowance and culminating in Transition, we can define seven distinct stages in any complete change process. Remember that the energy we are calling Chaos operates as a resistive force during each of these seven stages. Once a change process has traversed all seven of these stages, completing the cycle, a readiness exists for a new cycle of change to begin. And so a transition takes place between the seventh stage of one cycle (Transition) and the first stage of the next cycle (Allowance). Cycles of change may spiral one after another, as long as there is motivation or desire to drive the process.

This sequence of stages exists as potential everywhere in the world. But the potential can only be realized if enough desire or thrust exists to overcome resistance, pushing the process from one stage to the next. Even when a change process is initiated with a great deal of thrust behind it, the process may not be sustained. It can stall at any stage, and may even regress to earlier stages in the process. And so the sequence of stages from one through seven, and then on to the first stage of the next cycle, is not inevitable.

Completing a Change Cycle requires pushing through each stage of change through an act of will, and achieving a degree of change at each stage. To move from any given stage to the next, something must first have changed. Whether we are dealing with shifting ideas or viewpoints or with material change, an identifiable change occurs in the state of being of the subject at each stage in this process. What specifically changes is different at each stage. In a sense, we can view this whole process as a series of conflicts and resolutions. Although each change process is unique, characteristic patterns of conflict and resolution take place (or potentially take place) at each of the seven stages.

Conflict Resolution: The Creative Process

This conflict-resolution process has two opposing forces that vary at each stage. There is a driving force defined by the dominant energy of a given stage, and a resisting force called Chaos that must be overcome or reconciled in order to move from that stage of the change process to the next.

For example, the Allowance stage is characterized by the desire to take in or formulate new possibilities. This desire is the driving force that dominates Stage One. A counter force, Chaos, seeks at the same time to maintain the status quo. During the Allowance stage, Chaos acts as a force resisting the impulse to move beyond the existing concept, physical form, or system. A dynamic tension is set up between the energy of Allowance and the energy of Chaos during Stage One.

In order to move to Stage Two, Will, resolution between the two conflicting forces must be reached. This resolution process *is* the creative process—the means by which all directed movement and change occurs in the universe. This creative process can be seen operating at each stage of the change process, as well as on a large scale, between stages and between relatively independent cycles of change. This also implies that the four primary energies involved in the creative process—Allowance, Will, Capability, and Chaos—are present at each stage of the cycle. These energies are present, regardless of which energy form defines the dominant state of being, conflicts, and resolutions of that stage.

We can see that multiple forces are involved at each stage of the change process. Although one force dominates, the others are still vital to accomplish the desired change.

Scale

The Change Cycle model can be applied to all scales of change, from the microscopic to changes of cosmic proportion. I believe that the basic energies described here operate in all of our creative activities, as well as much change in the physical world that we don't directly affect.

Remember, too, that other sources of change exist, beyond the scope of this discussion. The focus of this book is on human will or desire, with an emphasis on understanding the dynamics of change as they apply to human endeavors. Thinking about change as it occurs mainly in human endeavor gives us a familiar reference point for grappling with and testing the validity and usefulness of these ideas.

Perspective

Just as the Change Cycle helps explain the creative process, it can also help explain other concepts. One such concept is stability. After reading the description of the eight energies of change, you might ask: "Where is the resting point?" From one perspective, there is none. If viewed from a distance, where your time frame is vastly expanded and the birth and death of individuals and ideas occur in but a moment of time, continual movement would be observable throughout the universe.

This would be true even though individuals living through a process of change could identify little or no movement, save for seemingly random fluctuations. The individuals living through such a process have a more limited perspective than is described here. They would view things primarily on the scale of their own life processes, or perhaps in terms of historical time frames. Thus, one might view life in terms of childhood, maturity, and old age, or perhaps think in terms of changes that have occurred within various decades of that life.

Similarly, one might view changes in the social systems of the world in terms of historical periods or even millennia. The scientist might expand this time frame to millions of years of human history or even to billions of years of earth history. The time frame could even be expanded to the moment of the big bang. Once we expand our time frame to this point, and imagine being able to hold this perspective and look out at the whole universe before our eyes, it isn't too difficult to imagine that the universe is continually in motion. When one collapses this perspective all the way down to that of the day-to-day existence of a human being, it may be much harder to imagine any continuous, directional movement of the universe.

Our perspective on the change process is profoundly influenced by our human perspective. We can often mistake random or momentary fluctuations for true directional change.
Conversely, we can also miss the grand sweeping changes
occurring all around us, simply because our point of reference
is too limited to observe them. So, from this grand perspective
we have alluded to, there is always movement. There is no
complete stability. The static state simply does not exist.

However, the grand perspective is not our usual way of looking
at events. When we focus our attention on the events and experiences that make up our daily lives, everything appears quite
different. On this stage of life, apparent movement and change
is all around us. And yet some things never appear to change
much. Neither your father's stubbornness nor the color of the
moss on your favorite tree appear to change noticeably over the
years.

We know about the aging process, both our own and
throughout nature. Surely these are real changes. And just as
surely, we can observe change in technology and the understanding of our world. Science and technology do advance, and
with them our notions of how we'd like to live, as well as of how
long we might live, also change. From our human perspective
these are real and significant changes. But the significance of
any change shifts as perspective shifts. Some changes that appear
to be important one moment turn out to be blips on the radar
screen of historical time. Other seemingly subtle or even unob-
served changes turn out to be early signs of major directional
shifts.

For our purposes, we need to distinguish between what seems
to be a significant change at one point in time and what proves
to be a significant change once we expand our time perspective.
This isn't to say that we will examine change only from the point
of view of the cosmic observer. It is saying, however, that many of
the perturbations that we observe may not prove to be the kind
of directional movement we are speaking of.

So, even though this directional movement occurs at all levels
of existence continuously, we can often be unaware of such
movement. Similarly, we can easily mistake a temporary but

relatively prominent shift for directional movement. The only way to avoid these errors in judgment is to expand one's time frame and to observe patterns of change from this broader perspective.

Why all this fuss to define directional movement? The reason is that change management is simplified and more effective if we can distinguish momentary fluctuations from directional change. The universe is filled with flux. Whether directed by human conscious will or derived from other sources, change is an ongoing occurrence, an inherent part of nature. The changes that arise, however, most often are not permanent shifts in state of being or direction, but temporary shifts without any identifiable causal agent or intent. Most of these changes will wash out or become insignificant over time.

Remember, in order to complete the seven stages in any cycle of directed change, there must be a driving force present throughout the entire process. If not, the process either will not be initiated or will bog down before completion. If the process bogs down before a shift in state of being occurs, there is no directional change, as defined here.

It is far more important to identify and manage directional shifts than changes that wash out in a short time. If we don't know what to filter from our thinking when attempting to manage change, it can seem like a confusing cacophony of noise that we encounter. Our minds are designed to recognize patterns and shifts in those patterns. If we are able to isolate a few key patterns that surround any area of desired change and to monitor them for significant shifts in direction, we can greatly simplify the process of change management. Once we focus our attention on a few significant patterns and track them over time, it becomes easier to distinguish directional shifts from less important, short-term shifts. These more permanent shifts are the ones critical to the strategic management of change. Once even one such directional shift in a key pattern has been identified, its implications can be vast. But first we must be able to sift through the vast flood of short-term flux and noise. From a practical standpoint, think of all the times you have seen a manager or organization respond to an event as though it were a harbinger of significant change, only to find it was a temporary aberration.

Changes in State of Being

For relatively permanent change to occur, a change must occur in the state of being of the subject—whether an idea, a person, an organization, a product, or anything else—and that change must prepare the way for subsequent directional changes that may occur in the next cycle.

A change in the subject's state of being is a relatively permanent shift in the dominant energy form affecting the subject. That is, if the state of being is defined at one point in time by the dominance, for example, of the energy of Connectedness, and a shift occurs so that the energy of Harmony or balance now dominates, there has been a shift in the subject's state of being.

Such changes pervade the entire being of the subject. If we are dealing with a person, the shift occurs in the nature of the driving force that underlies his or her values, behaviors, and thought patterns. If we are dealing with an idea, the shift that occurs will be in alignment with the basic underlying energy of the new stage.

Consider the idea of war. From the perspective of individual or collective Capability, there would be an emphasis on such aspects of war as the relative strength of forces arrayed on either side, or the effect of one technology or system of attack compared to another. There might be an emphasis on examining all aspects of war, in terms of the relative strength or power of each side, and on how to maximize one's effectiveness in winning. Many treatments of the subject of war are dominated by this perspective.

But if we shift perspectives to, let us say, Harmony, there would be a somewhat different emphasis in the aspects of war that were uppermost in interest. Certainly, any concept or treatment of war might include those aspects just mentioned. But the idea of war might also include notions of conflict resolution for the purpose of eventually creating greater unity among nations. Perhaps there would be greater emphasis on the behind-the-scenes negotiating and the resolution process that is part of the entire process of war.

Note that what has changed is not the actions that are part of making war. Rather, what has shifted is the perspective of the observer—in this case, the person who is thinking about war. The aspects of the phenomenon we call war that are of greatest interest have shifted. The concept of war has become more inclusive. If the concept of war has, in effect, transcended to the level of Harmony, it means that the concept now includes all aspects previously contained at the levels of being of Allowance, Will, Capability, and Connectedness. Added to those previously contained aspects are those that are freshly recognized and of the most compelling interest at the Harmony level of being.

In other words, as ideas evolve, they do not lose any of the meaning they had previously, but are enriched by the new and dominant point of view of the observer. As the perspective of the observer develops, so does every observation he or she makes. Nothing is really lost as his or her perspective on the world develops, but the relative value placed on various aspects of the experience shifts, as does the way all aspects are integrated with a concept. The observer becomes much more interested in some aspects of phenomena and less interested in others, which can lead to discoveries, most likely in the areas he or she is most interested in. These discoveries can lead to further refinement and eventually to a major shift in perspective, to the next level of being.

We have been dealing with how a concept or idea may change. Note that what has changed is the perspective and the under-standing of an observer, a conscious entity who formulates ideas about the world he or she experiences. The phenomenon (in this case, war) doesn't necessarily change. (The nature of war may or may not change; that's a separate question.) The concept of war changes, which immediately focuses our attention on the conscious entity who formulates the concept. Thus, the concept of war varies according to the observer and according to the observer's state of being. The observer's concept of war will shift as his or her own state of being shifts. So in the end, when we speak of the evolving nature of thought, we are really dealing with the evolving nature of the observer's state of being and accompanying perspective. Changing ideas implies changing perspectives. For an observer's perspective to truly change, a shift in his or her state of being is necessary.

This notion of the change process places emphasis on changes in the subject's state of being and on the perspective of the observer of phenomena. If a change occurs in either the state of being of subject or observer, then we may call this a true directional change. If, on the other hand, neither subject nor observer undergoes such a shift in state of being, then there has been no relatively permanent, directional shift. There can be no true directional change without a shift in state of being.

Natural Phenomena

Let's turn to a different arena, that of natural phenomena. Can the Change Cycle model be used to describe the natural change process? Let's start by looking at what happens in nature when there is no guiding influence from the seven fundamental energies. That is, what happens when Chaos, the eighth energy form, is dominant? Chaos provides resistance and adds definition to the other energies. We've seen how the resistance offered by Chaos plays out differently in each stage of the change process. Resistance, something that must be pushed against and overcome in order to move in a desired direction, remains a characteristic of Chaos, no matter how it plays out.

Throughout the seven stages of the change process, there is always a dynamic interaction between Chaos and the other energy forms. The most apparent (but not the only) way this manifests is in the specific issues or conflicts that exist at each stage. Generic dynamics describe how Chaos pushes against the dominant energy form of that stage—Allowance against Chaos, Will against Chaos, and so forth. In order to move through a given stage, the force of Chaos must be overbalanced or dominated by the other energy characteristic of that stage. This implies a persistence of drive or motivation in order to move through one stage and reach the next. In order to complete a cycle, there must be sufficient desire (another way of saying drive or motivation) present throughout the Change Cycle.

Now, what would happen if this drive was not present, if Chaos were the dominant energy form in a situation unopposed by the other energies? This condition can be observed in nature, where there isn't enough conscious driving force (manifesting as the other seven forces) to counteract the effects of Chaos. This condition manifests as the tendency toward disorder that we can observe throughout much of the natural world. Where there is insufficient conscious desire, as evidenced by the absence of the other seven energies, Chaos will dominate and result in increasing degrees of disorder.

Assuming this to be true, there are vast implications. In order to achieve directional, guided change, there must be a sufficient degree of consciousness and desire or will to drive the change process. Where there isn't sufficient willful consciousness, the change process as described earlier can't exist. Where in nature can we find such a "sufficient degree of willful consciousness"? We can certainly find it in human beings, but its existence elsewhere in our world is not as clear. There is no easily observable evidence of such willful consciousness in the non-living part of nature, nor in the plant kingdom. Among animal forms, we do see learning and conscious acts of will that seem to go beyond the realm of instinctive behavior or ontogenetic development.

While it may be possible that animals consciously create a change, within our own world, we find sufficient willful consciousness mainly—even if not exclusively—in human beings. The change processes we are discussing here do not include evolution as it occurs in nature, where a great deal of change can be explained through understanding how genetic heredity interacts with environment. Similarly, we aren't concerned with those aspects of nature where the entropic process dominates. Our interest here has been two major arenas where the process does apply and where human beings are involved directly: changes within ourselves and changes that we choose to make in the world around us.

Index